THE RISE OF GREAT BRITAIN

AN EIGHTEENTH-CENTURY VILLAGE INN

The Rise of Great Britain

1688-1837

R. J. UNSTEAD

with drawings by Stanley Herbert

LONDON
A & C BLACK LTD

A HISTORY OF BRITAIN

Also by R. J. Unstead

© 1963 A. & C. BLACK LTD.

4, 5 & 6 SOHO SQUARE, LONDON, W.I

REPRINTED WITH CORRECTIONS, 1964, 1967

MADE AND PRINTED IN GREAT BRITAIN BY
MORRISON AND GIBB LTD., LONDON AND EDINBURGH

FOREWORD

IN the five books of this series I have tried to describe simply the chief events and personalities in Britain's history so that they will interest the reader and help him to understand how and why certain happenings have taken place. Also, at a time when it is fashionable in some quarters to belittle Britain's achievements in the past and to doubt her place in the future, I have tried to show that whereas Britain has often acted foolishly or badly, her history shows the persistence of ideals which good men have lived by since Alfred's day.

In this story of a thousand years it is the character of a people that comes through; I hope that the reader will recognise this character and be glad.

R. J. Unstead

BONNIE PRINCE CHARLIE
AT HOLYROOD

CONTENTS

ACKNOWLEDGEMENTS

MOST of the drawings reproduced in this book are by Stanley
Herbert. The maps on pages 20, 50, 57 and 179 are by Cyril
Webber.

The illustrations on the cover, from *The Costume of Great
Britain* by W. H. Pyne (London, 1808), are reproduced by kind
permission of The Trustees of the British Museum.

Grateful acknowledgement is made to the following for their
permission to reproduce drawings and photographs: The
Trustees of the London Museum, pages 41 (a), 79, 120, 122 and
151; The Trustees of the British Museum, page 118; The
Trustees of the National Maritime Museum, page 128; The
National Portrait Gallery, pages 41 (b), 61 (a), 71, 107 (a, b
and c), 109 (a), 137, 150, 198, 201 (b), 206 (a) and 216; The
Mansell Collection, pages 27, 44, 73, 76, 115 (b), 116 (a), 119,
123, 129, 154 (a and b), 182, 199 (a), 210, 212 and 213; The
United States Information Service, pages 138, 141, 143 (a and b),
146 and 147.

The illustrations on pages 9 (b), 127 and 145 are from *Travel
by Sea* by Robert J. Hoare; those on pages 12, 13 (a), 14,
15 (b), 22, 25, 33, 37, 49 and 155 are from *Historic Costume* by
Lucy Barton; on pages 43 (a) and 94 (b) from *Social Life in
England* Book 3 by John Finnemore; on pages 10 (a and b),
11 (b), 29, 50 (b) and 156 from *Looking at History* Book 3 by
R. J. Unstead; on pages 62, 67, 92, 121, 124, 125, 131 (b),
132, 168, 172, 181, 202, 205 and 206 (b) from *Looking at
History* Book 4 by R. J. Unstead; on pages 19 and 39 from
English Costume of the Seventeenth Century by Iris Brooke; on
page 94 (a) from *London* by John Hayes; on pages 42 and 43
from *A History of Houses* by R. J. Unstead; on pages 99 and
100 (a and b) from *The Story of the Theatre* by David Male;
on page 32 from *Black's Children's Encyclopaedia*; on page 96
from *Travel by Road* by R. J. Unstead; on pages 68 and 88 from
Georgian Grace by John Gloag; on pages 54 (a) and 59 from
A General History of England 1688–1832 by Barker, St. Aubyn &
Ollard; on pages 38, 54 (b) and 70 from *People in History* Book
4 by R. J. Unstead; on pages 159 (a and b), 160, 162, 163
and 167 (a and b) from *La Révolution Française* by Thiers; on
pages 173, 177, 183, 184, 186, 187, 188, 189, 190 (b), 191 and
192 from *The Life of Napoleon Bonaparte* by S. Baring-Gould;
on page 89 from *London in the 18th Century* by Sir Walter Besant;
on pages 156 and 217 from *Reed's History Notebooks*; on page 215
from *Looking at East Africa: the 19th Century* by John Osogo.
The drawing on page 9 (a) is by J. C. B. Knight and that on
page 165 by S. A. Edwards.

JAMES II LANDS
IN FRANCE

PART ONE

FROM 1688 TO 1763

CHAPTER I

THE SETTLEMENT OF 1688

ON Christmas Day 1688, in the early hours of the morning, King James II of England stepped from a fishing-smack on to the shore of France. He looked tired and ill, but his bedraggled air was hardly to be wondered at. In a few weeks of topsy-turvy confusion, he had lost his kingdom without a hand being raised to help him.

" The Glorious Revolution " which had unseated James II was, in fact, a most inglorious affair, besmirched by treachery and by zeal to join the winning side. But at least the Protestant religion had been saved without bloodshed.

James was a failure. He lacked the charm of his father, Charles I, and the craftiness of his brother, Charles II. Like them, he meant to be a king who did not

9

CHARLES II'S
YACHT

JAMES II

answer to Parliament, but, unlike either, he made it perfectly clear that he also intended to restore the Roman Catholic religion. He never understood that Englishmen would put up with kings who were surly, dishonest, immoral or mad, but only as long as they were Protestants.

When it came to the pinch, James, once a capable admiral, lacked courage and decision. He loved his navy but could not make men love him, so his disloyal captains and their timid admiral allowed the Dutch ships to reach Torbay as if an English fleet never existed. He had assembled an army to awe the Londoners, but he failed to use it to attack the Dutchman as soon as he had got ashore. Days later, when he did move, he was delayed by a severe nose-bleed at Salisbury. When he was better he found that his best general, John Churchill, his leading officers and his own nephew had gone over to the other side. Back in London, he learned that his second daughter, the princess Anne, had also deserted him and, in the confusion of rumour and fear, his nerve broke and he fled.

James could not even make a success of running away. A rabble of Kentish fishermen caught him and hustled him to Faversham, knocking him about and even tearing his breeches to see if there were jewels hidden in the seams. Taken back to London, he had to be allowed to escape again, with an escort of Dutch soldiers to make sure he did so properly and in time to allow his son-in-law, William of Orange, to ride in from Windsor, up Piccadilly and into the capital.

WILLIAM OF
ORANGE

In London, the position was delicate. Only the King could summon Parliament and he had gone, taking the Great Seal with him. But legal points of this kind never worried Englishmen, and a Parliament was hastily gathered to solve the problem of the vacant throne.

A PARLIA-
MENT WAS
GATHERED
TO SOLVE
THE
PROBLEM
OF THE
VACANT
THRONE

The Tories found themselves in a difficult situation, for they had been brought up to believe in the Divine Right of kings (i.e. that kings were appointed to rule by God). They could only justify their disloyalty to James by convincing themselves that he had driven them to it. If he were recalled, would he keep any promises, would the Church of England be safe? If he abdicated, would William consent to be Regent? Could his wife, Mary, the daughter of James, become Queen, with William holding the reins?

The arguments went to and fro until William settled them all. He allowed it to be known that he had no intention of becoming his wife's subject; he was quite ready to go back to Holland and to leave the English to their problems. At this, the waverers swallowed their doubts and William and Mary became joint sovereigns.

THE SETTLEMENT

Although his mother was an English princess, William of Orange had little interest in England or its people. He came to secure the forces and money he needed to defend his beloved Holland from the grasp of Louis XIV of France. But, as an honourable

MARY

11

AN ELEGANT
COURT LADY

man, William was prepared to make a bargain and to do his duty.

Unfortunately, " Dutch Billy " had no winning ways. He said little and smiled not at all, weighing up men in a dry cold silence which made them uncomfortable at the time and angry afterwards. In appearance, he was a little scrap of a man, bony and mis-shapen, yet with an inner toughness that kept him going through campaigns and sieges. Naturally, his silences were mistaken for rudeness and he did not help matters by seeming to dislike Englishmen and by making lavish gifts to his Dutch friends. At Court, the ladies sneered at his lack of gallantry, for he had no time for fashionable gossip and, like such men, was probably half-afraid of elegant women.

Yet England needed William ; he was never liked, but many came to respect his dogged spirit and, for his part, " the low Dutch bear ", as the ladies called him, needed England if Holland was to survive.

William and Mary became joint-sovereigns by the *Bill of Rights* : the King, who must be a Protestant, was not to set aside the laws as James II had done ; he could not raise taxes or maintain an Army without Parliament's consent. For the moment, however, the Army could not be disbanded because of the danger of a French invasion. Therefore, by the *Mutiny Act*,

The supremacy of Parliament

troops could be kept under military discipline for one year only, and this made it certain that Parliament must meet to renew the Act year by year.

To prevent parliaments from remaining in existence too long, the *Triennial Act* (1694) called for a General Election after three years at most. Taxation was to be considered every year, when the King's ministers were to bring their estimates of money required to the House of Commons. Then the House would debate the matter and decide upon the taxes for the coming year. This was the origin of the modern " Budget ".

Almost the first measure in the Settlement was the passing of a *Toleration Act* (1689) to reward the Dissenters (also called " Nonconformists ") for standing firm when James II had promised them religious liberty in order to grant it also to Catholics. Dissenters were to be allowed to worship in their own meeting-houses, but they were still barred from the universities and from important posts in the service of the Government and Crown.

As far as Roman Catholics were concerned, William did not share the popular loathing of their religion ; he could not secure toleration for them, but he managed to see that they were not persecuted as long as they kept quiet.

MEN STILL
WORE WIGS

Finally, some years later, in 1701, after Mary had died without children and her sister Anne's little son had also died, Parliament arranged for the Succession by means of the *Act of Settlement*. It was decided that the heir to the throne, after Princess Anne, should be Sophia of Hanover, daughter of Elizabeth, the beautiful daughter of James I who long ago in 1613 had married a German Prince called the Elector Palatine. Sophia was the nearest Protestant of the royal line, and although she did not live to reach the throne of England, her son was to be George I, the first of the Hanoverian kings.

DISSENTERS WERE
TO BE ALLOWED
TO WORSHIP IN
THEIR OWN
MEETING HOUSES

IN DEFENCE OF THE SETTLEMENT : SCOTLAND

Under Charles II and James II, Scotland's fortunes had sunk low. The former tyranny of the Kirk (the Church) was exchanged for the tyranny of a set of nobles notorious for their drunkenness and evil ways.

The Covenant was thrown aside, bishops were restored and the clergy were no longer appointed by their congregatons. One-third of all the ministers, mainly those in the south-west, were " outed " and were replaced by curates who were often quite unsuitable persons.

These were " the Killing Times ", when Graham of Claverhouse, afterwards Viscount Dundee, saw to it that his dragoons broke up the meetings of devout Presbyterians and shot down Covenanters at their meetings among the hills.

The flight of James II ended the power of the Council, and a Scottish Parliament offered the crown to William and Mary on condition that the Presbyterian Church be restored.

Viscount Dundee raised an army of Highlanders, hoping to embarrass the government until James II arrived with an army from France. William sent General Mackay north with Scottish regiments from Holland, and the two forces met in the Pass of *Killiecrankie* in July 1689. The Highlanders tore down upon Mackay's regulars and routed them in one terrible charge, but the bullet that killed Dundee made *Dundee's rising* their victory useless. With no one to lead them, the clansmen soon drifted back to their mountain homes, taking with them the legend of " Bonnie Dundee ". A victory for the Covenanters at *Dunkeld* ended the danger from Scotland.

Two years later occurred a tragic sequel to this short campaign. William had agreed that the Scottish Parliament should be independent and that those who

CLAVERHOUSE'S DRAGOONS
BREAK UP A PRESBY-
TERIAN GATHERING

had fought against him should be pardoned, provided they took an oath of loyalty by December 31st 1691.

All the chiefs took the oath, except MacIan, chief of the Macdonalds at Glencoe. He purposely delayed until the last minute and then arrived at Fort William, whose commander sent him on to Inveraray. Delayed by snow, MacIan did not take the oath until January 7th, one week late.

Sir John Dalrymple, the King's Scottish adviser, had a grudge against the Macdonalds, and he obtained royal permission to punish them for their chief's delay. William signed the order, but whether he read it or understood what was intended is doubtful.

On February 1st a Captain Campbell arrived at Glencoe with 120 soldiers and asked for quarters. The visitors were treated as guests and then, in the dark hours of February 13th the Campbells rose and killed all their hosts, except the few who fled into the snow-bound hills.

In a cruel age, the treachery of the *Massacre of Glencoe* might have passed unnoticed. But Dalrymple and William had enemies who made certain that the horrible affair was brought to light. An enquiry was held, Dalrymple resigned, but William refused to punish anyone.

AN ENGLISH
OFFICER

15

The crime was planned by a Scot and was committed by Scots against their countrymen. But the King of England had signed the order and William, usually more lenient than most, was thus the cause of lasting bitterness in the Highlands. Glencoe helped to keep alive a passionate loyalty to the House of Stuart.

IN DEFENCE OF THE SETTLEMENT : IRELAND

Despite the tragedy of Glencoe, the Revolution of 1688 gave back to Scotland the religion that the majority of her people wanted, and more parliamentary freedom than they had hoped for. The fate of Ireland was different.

James II in Ireland

Three months after his flight to France, where Louis XIV generously installed him in a palace at St. Germain, James II was in Dublin.

The Irish had no particular love for the Stuarts, but if they supported a Catholic King, they could hope to overthrow the Protestants who had taken half their land. For James, Ireland was the base from which he could win back his kingdom.

Neither Louis XIV nor William wished to waste time in Ireland when both knew that the real struggle must be fought on the continent. Louis gave James money, supplies and a few officers to help organise the Irish who had already taken up arms and had driven the Protestants into Londonderry and Enniskillen. For 105 days, the Protestants held out in Londonderry against a huge ill-armed force under the Earl of Tyrconnel. Food became so scarce that dogs, horses and even rats and salt hides were eaten, but the garrison beat off every attack with the desperate courage

THE MASSACRE OF GLENCOE

THE SIEGE OF LONDONDERRY

that sprang from knowledge of what their fate would be if the enemy got in or if they surrendered. At last, food-ships from London burst the boom across the river and the starving defenders were relieved. Meanwhile, at Enniskillen, the Protestants had broken out to drive off their attackers.

In 1690 William himself crossed into Ireland. Action was essential, for the Whigs and Tories at home were quarrelling, the country was uneasy and every other Englishman of any importance was in secret touch with the Jacobites, which was the name given to the supporters of the Stuarts.

Gathering up some northern troops, William marched towards Dublin and found his father-in-law's army drawn up beyond the River Boyne. Throwing caution aside for once, William ordered his foreign regulars to ford the river and attack. The *Battle of the Boyne* was decisive, not so much because the Irish were defeated, but because James again lost his nerve. Before the battle was over, he galloped off to Dublin and soon afterwards took ship to France.

Defeat of the Jacobites

Southern Ireland held out for another year, but

then Marlborough captured Cork, and Limerick surrendered on the promise of fair terms.

By the *Treaty of Limerick* (1691), the Irish Catholics were to have the same freedoms as in the reign of Charles II, but once the surrender had been made, the treaty was shamefully torn up.

The Protestants in the Irish Parliament passed a number of laws known as *The Penal Code* and which were designed to crush the Catholics for ever. All the priests were banished, Roman Catholics were forbidden to teach in schools or in private, to carry arms, to own a decent horse or to leave all their property to their eldest sons. These laws and many more brought trade, education and progress to a standstill. For a time the Irish lost the spirit and will to help the Stuarts or to rebel against their oppressors. Only deep and sullen hatred was left.

CHAPTER 2

THE WARS AGAINST LOUIS XIV

1. The War of the League of Augsberg, 1689–1697

FROM his vast palace at Versailles, built for him by the toil of thirty thousand half-starved Frenchmen, Louis ruled France like an emperor. Untroubled by parliaments, unconcerned about his people, he raised armies and fleets, made the laws and imposed the taxes for the glorification of France, which, as he said, was himself.

The finest artists and musicians, the generals, admirals and engineers, as well as the entire aristocracy, were summoned to Versailles to attend at Court. The most highly privileged were allowed to be present when His Majesty arose from his bed each morning ; the others awaited his commands, hovering about the throne in brilliant idleness to form a background for the greatest showman in Europe.

To strengthen France, Louis planned to extend her borders to the River Rhine. He would have to conquer Holland and the Spanish Netherlands ; he was certain to alarm Austria and Germany as well, and it was unlikely that England would tamely allow the Netherlands to become part of France and a perpetual threat to her trade and safety.

In the path of Louis XIV's ambition stood the puny figure of William of Orange. To save Holland, he had gone to England, and once he had secured his new kingdom, he turned back to his life's task of repelling the French invader. Steadily, he succeeded in weaving an alliance against the Grand Monarch. It was called the *League of Augsberg*, and its members, Holland, England, Sweden, Spain, several German

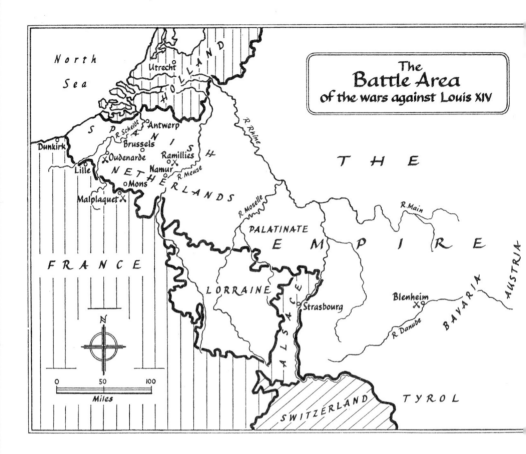

The Battle Area of the wars against Louis XIV

princedoms and Austria, were united, not in friendship or religion, but in fear of France.

The War of the League of Augsberg began badly. The French were superior at sea, and in June 1690, a fortnight after William landed in Ireland, they defeated *A naval defeat* the English fleet at the *Battle of Beachy Head*, and so won command of the Channel.

Fortunately, the French did not realise how great their victory was. They let slip the opportunity to strangle English trade, to prevent the movement of English troops by sea, and to keep England in a fever of alarm against invasion.

Not until 1692 did a French army of invasion

20

stand on the coast of Normandy, with a French fleet ready to clear the Channel. But the English had already recovered. They drove the French warships back and forced them to fight close to their own shore. Some escaped, but the rest were driven ashore and burnt at the water's edge before the mournful eyes of James II.

The *Battle of La Hogue* was as decisive as Trafalgar. The French lost only about fifteen first-class ships, hardly more than the English losses at Beachy Head, but whereas England had set to work to build up her fleet again, France now fell back on defence. Her Navy could no longer support an invasion or challenge her enemy in direct battle. Command of the sea passed to England and, with it, command of much of the world's trade, and from this trade came the money to win a long drawn-out war.

England wins back her control of the seas

On land, the war was fought in the Netherlands. It was a war of moves and counter-moves, of sieges and withdrawals, in country bristling with such fortress-towns as Mons, Lille and Namur.

William was an expert in this kind of dogged warfare, but the war was costly and the gains were few, so the English grumbled and liked their silent king even less.

But Louis XIV had his troubles too. Greed and extravagance were destroying the wealth of France, and her overseas trade had well-nigh collapsed.

THE ENGLISH
FLEET DROVE
THE FRENCH
WARSHIPS CLOSE
TO THE SHORE

Exhaustion on both sides brought the war to an end at the *Treaty of Ryswick* (1697), when Louis agreed to recognise William as King of England (Mary had died three years earlier) and promised to give no more help to James II. The Dutch were to keep troops in the Barrier Fortresses* and Louis handed back almost all the territory he had won. On balance, William had triumphed, for Holland still stood, and England was once again a great Power.

ENGLISH POLITICS

The two political parties in England were the Whigs and the Tories. Both got their names from the contemptuous gibes of their opponents ; the Whigs were said to be " whiggamores ", rascally Scottish horse-drovers, while " tories " was an old name for Irish robbers. This was a time when few men in politics were honest, when men high in the Government and in royal service gave and took bribes, wrote letters to the Jacobite exiles in France, changed parties and generally conducted themselves in ways that would be considered disgraceful nowadays.

It was the Whigs who had taken the lead in inviting William III to England. Apart from some of the great landowners and many yeomen farmers, Whigs were mostly townsmen—merchants, lawyers, bankers, shopkeepers—engaged in business and trade. Their fathers and grandfathers had been on the side of Hampden and Pym against the King, and their money and broadswords had helped to bring victory to Cromwell. Many had been brought up in the Puritan faith, so the rank and file of Whig supporters included many Dissenters who wanted toleration for all forms of Protestant worship, but none at all for

A YEOMAN
FARMER

* These were fortresses in the Spanish Netherlands along the French frontier, in which the Dutch were allowed to keep troops.

THE WHIGS
WHO TOOK
THE LEAD IN
INVITING
WILLIAM III
BACK TO
ENGLAND
WERE MOSTLY
TOWNSMEN
ENGAGED
IN BUSINESS
OR TRADE

Roman Catholics. Needless to say, the Whigs were strong Parliament-men and highly suspicious of any increase in the powers of the King. Yet they found themselves supporting William and his war in the Netherlands. They had turned James II off his throne, and the war was being fought, in part, to prevent him coming back. Furthermore, as businessmen, they were gaining most from England's improved trade and from the manufactures of war.

The Tories took the opposite line in almost everything. They were mostly country-dwellers—squires, parsons, and the landed gentry who had been the backbone of the Cavalier cause. They believed in absolute loyalty to the King and to the Church of England, but they were constantly finding themselves in embarrassing positions. Many still felt guilty about deserting the rightful king, and it would not have taken much cleverness on the part of James II to win them back. They hated William and his Dutch friends, and they resented paying land-tax to support *Tories in* a war which they believed was none of England's *difficulties* business. Yet, although the Tories were the " peace party ", no patriotic squire wanted to see his own country defeated ; he felt no kindness towards the

23

Dissenters but he feared the Roman Catholics much more. He believed that James was king by Divine Right, but he could not support a king who might destroy the Church of England.

In this situation, William soon learned to steer a course between the rival parties. He naturally favoured the Whigs who had invited him over and who were finding most of the money for the war, but he was careful not to drive the Tories into such despair that they would welcome James II at any price.

Money matters   The huge cost of the war brought about two important changes in the management of the country's money affairs. In the past, kings had borrowed for their wars and had paid back when taxes came in, but now the cost was too great for the royal purse. So Montagu, the Whig Chancellor, arranged that the Government should borrow money and promise to pay interest on the loans. Thus, a man could lend a large sum and be certain that he would receive a regular income year in and year out. If he wanted his money back, he had only to sell his " Government Stock " (i.e. the documents which stated the amount of the loan) to someone else. The Government was, and still is, permanently in debt but the promise to pay the interest could be relied on. These vast sums lent to the Government became known as *The National Debt*, and it was clear that William soon had a large class of rich men permanently interested in keeping the Stuarts away, since, if they came back, Government Stock would be worthless.

The second measure was the opening of the *Bank of England* in 1694. William Paterson, a Scot, put forward the idea of a private company which would lend money to the Government and generally help the flow of business deals where very large sums of money were involved. The Tories tried their best to

overthrow this Whiggish scheme, but the Bank succeeded and soon played an important part in England's
widening trade.   One of the Bank's useful activities
was the issue of " bank notes " which were convenient
to use, and which could be exchanged for gold whenever necessary.

2. The War of the Spanish Succession. 1702–1713

A FRENCH
COURT LADY
WEARING A
MASK

The Treaty of Ryswick was no more than a four-
year breathing-spell in which Louis and William
repaired their finances and laid their plans for the
Spanish crisis which was fast approaching.

The greatness of Spain had declined during the
previous half-century, but she still possessed an enormous empire overseas and many territories in Europe.
Her king, Charles II, had come to the throne when he
was four years old, so sickly and deformed that no one
expected him to live for long.   Actually, he had
survived for another thirty-five years, keeping half
of Europe on tenterhooks about the succession.

By 1697 it was clear that the Spanish King would
not last much longer and, since he had no children, the
question arose as to who should succeed him.   One of
his sisters had married Louis XIV and his other
sister had married Leopold of Austria, the Holy
Roman Emperor*.   Since both sisters had children,
there were three great-nephews with good claims to
the throne of Spain.   They were Philip of Anjou
(Louis XIV's grandson), Charles, Archduke of Austria,
and a little boy who was Electoral Prince of Bavaria.

*The claimants to
the throne*

The problem was not to decide which of these
princes had the best claim, but which one would be

* The Holy Roman Empire had existed for nearly 900 years ; it
was a union of numerous German kingdoms whose rulers elected
an Emperor.   For centuries they had elected the Archdukes of
Austria, members of the Hapsburg family.

allowed to gain so rich an inheritance. France would
not let Austria have the Spanish Empire, while
Austria and most of the other Powers were terrified at
the thought of France becoming more powerful than
all the rest of Europe put together.

*Louis XIV and
William solve
the problem*

Louis and William decided to solve the problem in
their own way. Without consulting anyone, they
awarded the lion's share to the little Prince of Bavaria,
with smaller pickings for both France and Austria.
This was the *First Partition Treaty* (1698), and it came
to nothing because the little boy died within a few
months. The two wily kings tried again, and by the
Second Partition Treaty (1700), they decided that France
and Austria should share the Spanish possessions more
or less equally.

When the news got out, the King of Spain and his
people were furious at the plan to carve up their
empire. Charles II made a will leaving all his dominions to Philip of Anjou. If he refused, they were all to
go to Charles of Austria. Having settled his affairs, the
Spanish king died.

A SAILOR

The prize proved too tempting for Louis XIV.
When he learned that his own grandson was to succeed
to the throne of Spain, he decided to support the dead
man's will and to take no further interest in the
arrangement he had made with William. William
was horrified. His life's work was ruined if Louis and
his family were to possess not only France and Spain,
but the Netherlands, most of Italy and a vast empire
overseas. Holland and England, too, would be
doomed.

But, for the moment, the English and most of the
Dutch people were blind to the danger. They had
had enough of war, and in England the Tories were
now in command, resolved to let continental affairs
settle themselves.

However, as in 1688, Louis acted rashly when

success was within his grasp.   Instead of allowing events to take their course as quietly as possible, he seized the Dutch Barrier Fortresses, announced that France would have sole right to trade with the Spanish dominions and that his grandson Philip was not debarred from the French throne merely because he had now gained the Spanish one.   As though this were not enough, Louis next made certain that England should be as alarmed as Holland had now become. When James II died in 1701 he recognised the late king's son as " James III of England ".   The English had no love for William III, but they were not having a Catholic king chosen for them by Louis XIV.   Tories and Whigs alike clamoured for war.

While he was still re-shaping the Grand Alliance against France, William suffered a riding accident. His horse stumbled on a mole-hill and the King was thrown, breaking his collar-bone.   Campaigns and ceaseless work in two kingdoms had drained his strength and weakened his lungs.   In his poor health, the mishap proved fatal, and in March 1702, William III died and was succeeded by his wife's sister, Anne.

THE GREAT DUKE OF MARLBOROUGH

Queen Anne was an amiable woman married to a pleasant duffer, George of Denmark.   Her closest friend had long been Sarah Churchill, the masterful Duchess of Marlborough, whose control of Anne had kept the Duke out of the limelight.

Anne was a Tory, surrounded by friends who did not hide their contempt for William.   She and her sister Mary had not been on speaking terms for years, and although John Churchill, Duke of Marlborough, had done much to ensure the bloodless success of the 1688 Revolution, William never trusted him.   However, he recognised Marlborough's ability, and named

QUEEN ANNE

him to take command in the coming struggle against Louis XIV.

A great soldier

Only Wellington on land and Nelson at sea can rank with Marlborough as a commander. Immensely ambitious for fame and wealth, charming and patient with his allies, beloved by his soldiers and a legend to his enemies, he equalled William as a diplomat and outshone him as a general.

His task was immense. Louis XIV had taken the Spanish Netherlands and Northern Italy, and he naturally had his grandson's kingdom of Spain on his side. Where William had had the advantage of his name and royal rank, Marlborough as a mere English noble had to hold together an alliance of argumentative Dutch, of quarrelsome Germans and proud Austrians.

When he arrived in the Netherlands in 1702, Marlborough found that the French had already invaded Holland, but by masterly manoeuvres he forced them back. During the next year, little was achieved, since the " field deputies ", a committee of Dutch civilians, would not allow Marlborough to risk their troops in direct attacks. Meanwhile, an English fleet, after failing in an attack on *Cadiz*, sunk a Spanish treasure fleet in Vigo Bay, and won over Portugal to the Grand Alliance ; Admiral Rooke captured *Gibraltar* (1704) and battered the French Fleet at the *Battle of Malaga*.

Marlborough's greatest victory occurred far away from the Low Countries. The Elector of Bavaria had joined Louis XIV and, with French support, intended to capture Vienna. This would knock Austria out of

MARLBOROUGH
ON CAMPAIGN

AFTER THE BATTLE OF BLENHEIM
THE FRENCH COMMANDER
SURRENDERS HIS SWORD TO THE
DUKE OF MARLBOROUGH

the war and leave Louis free to concentrate all his forces against the Netherlands.

Marlborough realised the danger, but he also knew that the English and Dutch governments would not allow him to move from the Netherlands. He therefore decided to act without orders. Suddenly making for the Rhine, he was in Bavaria before anyone realised what was happening. Marching at a speed which only the greatest generals can exact from their troops, he joined forces with his friend Prince Eugene, the Austrian commander, and presently came upon the French and Bavarian armies drawn up in a strong position along a stream that flows into the River Danube, near to the village of *Blenheim*.

Declaring, " I rely on the bravery and discipline of the troops, which will make amends for our disadvantages ", Marlborough made a frontal attack, himself commanding the cavalry, unusually placed in the centre. While Eugene pressed on the right, Marlborough crossed the swampy ground with difficulty, burst through the centre and wheeled left to roll up the French wing at the village of Blenheim. The enemy broke. While the Bavarians retreated, 14,000 Frenchmen were killed or drowned in the Danube ; 11,000 were captured, with over 100 guns. Vienna was saved, Bavaria was out of the war and the

The Battle of Blenheim 1704

29

French had to retire from Germany. Though the war was to last for several years longer, Marlborough had changed its course.

The people of England went mad with joy. Marlborough was rewarded with a fortune and a great estate where the immense palace of Blenheim was later to be built in his honour. The delight of the Queen knew no bounds, and it was plain to all that Duchess Sarah virtually ruled the kingdom.

Next year, the Dutch civilians were again able to prevent Marlborough from making any decisive moves, but in 1706, he thrashed Marshall Villeroi at *Ramillies*, and Prince Eugene drove the French from Northern Italy. At this high-water mark of success, peace could have been made, but greed and dissension among the Allies prolonged the war for seven more years.

In 1708 Marlborough, the general who never lost a battle or failed to take a fortress, won the *Battle of Oudenarde* and captured *Lille*. The road to Paris seemed to be open. France was almost on her knees, her Treasury was empty, her armies were shattered, and her people near to starvation. When Louis asked for peace the Allies informed him that he must drive his own grandson Philip from the Spanish throne. To this, the old king replied, " If I have to fight, I would rather fight my enemies than my children."

" I would rather fight my enemies "

As always, the French soldiers rallied to defend their native land. Forced to retreat after the *Battle of Malplaquet* (1709), they inflicted such enormous losses on Marlborough's army that the glory of the great general was dimmed, and the war reverted to a series of sieges and manoeuvres. It was Marlborough's last battle.

THE TORIES IN POWER

Marlborough had been kept in his command by the Whigs. But England was now tired of the war whose cost increased as its glories faded. The Queen, too, was weary of Duchess Sarah's over-bearing tyranny, and she began to show favour to Mrs. Masham, a soothing respectful lady with high Tory connections.

The anti-war party worked up public indignation. The war, they said, was being run for Marlborough's benefit ; he was setting himself up as a second Cromwell by asking to be made Captain-General for life ; England was paying the Allies and fighting the battles. When a clergyman named Sacheverell was prosecuted for preaching a sermon against the Whigs, the mob made him into a popular hero and a general election returned a large majority of Tories to Parliament. After a furious quarrel, the Queen plucked up sufficient courage to dismiss the Duchess Sarah. The fall of Marlborough followed.

Charged with receiving a commission of £60,000 on the supply of bread for the Army, and with helping himself to a quarter of a million pounds intended as pay for foreign troops, Marlborough was dismissed from his command. Shortly afterwards, London witnessed the shameful sight of hooligans running after the great general's coach with shouts of " Stop thief ! "

Marlborough in disgrace

The argument about Marlborough's character has never been settled. Some have accused him of greed and treachery, while others, notably his descendant, Sir Winston Churchill, hold that his actions were no different from those of other men in high office, that the money he was supposed to have taken was properly spent on his secret service and that he showed steadfast loyalty to his Queen and to the Allied cause. At all events, he was one of the greatest commanders in history.

End of the war

The Tories, led by Robert Harley and Henry St. John, withdrew the British army from the war, and this compelled the Dutch to agree to a peace. In 1713, England, Holland and the minor powers signed the *Treaty of Utrecht* with France. Archduke Charles of Austria, who had become Emperor Charles VI, was indignant that the Allies had not placed him on the throne of Spain, but, within a year, he, too, signed the treaty.

The peace which settled the map of Europe until the French Revolution, gave France better terms than she could have expected after Ramillies and Oudenarde. Louis kept some small additions to his boundaries and his grandson remained King of Spain, but France was so impoverished by the wars and her armies so discredited by Marlborough's fame, that she was unable to upset Europe again until the advent of Napoleon.

Holland recovered its safety and its fortresses, but the long struggle for freedom had so exhausted the small country that it never again became the major Power that it had been in the 17th century. Austria gained Milan, Naples and the Netherlands in exchange for Charles's claim to Spain, where Philip V retained his crown.

Great Britain gained Gibraltar and Minorca, Nova Scotia and the Hudson Bay territory. By an agreement called the *Assiento*, she also obtained the right to supply negroes to Spanish America.

More important than these gains, Great Britain's prestige had risen immensely high. As in 1815 and 1945, it was recognised that British wealth, her Navy and the genius of one man, backed by a stubborn nation, had saved Europe from being dominated by a military Power.

BUYING AND SELLING SLAVES

THE UNION WITH SCOTLAND

Though still unfamiliar, the term " Great Britain " *" Great Britain "*
now began to be used, for in 1707 England and
Scotland were joined under one Government.

The two countries had had the same King since
James I's accession, but, apart from a short period in
Cromwell's time, they had kept their separate
parliaments, laws, churches and trade. It was a
commercial disaster that hastened the Union, for the
Scots, barred from English trade overseas, invested
heavily in a project known as *The Darien Scheme*
(1695-99), which was formed to bring Eastern trade
across the Isthmus of Darien (Panama). The scheme
failed through inexperience and because Spanish
protests caused William III to withdraw its charter.
At the time, William could not afford to quarrel with
Spain, and he realised that union between the two
countries was the only way of avoiding these unhappy
complications.

William's poor health and his concentration on
European affairs caused the matter to be left over
until Queen Anne's reign. The Scots, sore about their
money losses and anxious for their Presbyterian
Church, were offended that England had fixed the
succession without consulting them. Such a situation
was so obviously to Louis XIV's liking that both sides
swallowed their pride and came to terms.

It was agreed that Scotland should keep her own
Church and Law, should send Members to Parliament
at Westminster and should have equal trading
rights. On May 1st 1707 the United Kingdom
of Great Britain came into existence.

DOWNFALL OF THE TORIES

With Marlborough in disgrace and a peace treaty
safely signed, it seemed as if the Tories were in office

AN ANGLICAN BISHOP
WEARING A PERUKE

Bolingbroke plans to seize power

for many years. But their leaders, Harley, Earl of Oxford, and St. John, who was made Viscount Bolingbroke, soon proved to be rivals instead of partners. Bolingbroke, brilliant and hungrily ambitious, planned to seize power by a masterful stroke.

It was clear that Queen Anne had not long to live. She was only forty-eight, but her health had never been robust, and the death of all her seventeen children not only depressed her spirits but made her feel that God had punished her for deserting her father, James II. More and more she grew to detest the idea of her German cousin inheriting the crown, and her mind turned constantly towards her half-brother, James " the Third ", whose birth had led directly to the 1688 Revolution.

While the Whigs were assuring George of Hanover that he would have their support, the Tories were in touch with the exiled James. They told him that he must make at least a show of conforming to the Church of England, but to his credit, James would not budge from his own religion beyond promising liberty to Protestants.

Bolingbroke now set his plan into motion. While Oxford and the moderate Tories shilly-shallied, he bribed Mrs. Masham, the Queen's companion, to influence her royal mistress against Oxford. Then he began to plan the removal of Whigs from every position of importance in politics, in the law courts and in the Army. They were to be replaced by " High ", i.e. extreme, Tories, and there is little doubt that he would have offered the crown to James.

In 1714 Bolingbroke played his trump cards. To win over the Church of England supporters, the Schism Act * was introduced to prevent Dissenters

* Schism, pronounced " sizm ", means a separation in a Church. The Act forbade anyone to keep a school unless he were a member of the Church of England. It was repealed in 1717.

from educating their children. Next, in July, the Queen suddenly dismissed Oxford, and Bolingbroke had a free hand. He needed only a few weeks to put his own supporters in all the key positions in the Government. But the excitement of the plot was too much for the ailing Queen. Within forty-eight hours of dismissing Oxford, she had a stroke, and two days later she died.

Bolingbroke had not completed his Cabinet, and the Duke of Shrewsbury, to whom the dying Queen had handed the Lord Treasurer's staff (there was no office of Prime Minister yet), acted promptly but not for Bolingbroke. The Elector of Hanover was proclaimed King George I, and soon afterwards *The Whig* Bolingbroke was dismissed. He fled abroad to the *triumph* Jacobite Court, where his abilities were never made use of and, though he was one day to be allowed to return to England, his career was ruined.

Once again the Whigs had triumphed, bringing in the monarch of their choice, and for more than fifty years the Tories were to remain out of office.

LOUIS XIV

CHAPTER 3

THE RULE OF WALPOLE

THE GERMAN KING

A German King

GEORGE I was fifty-four when he became King of Great Britain, and although he had known for years that he would inherit his mother Sophia's claim, he had not bothered to learn to speak English. He much preferred his own little kingdom of Hanover, where he was absolute ruler and where the obedient people contrasted favourably, in his view, with the pugnacious English.

Since George could only talk to his ministers in French, he was able to take little part in the day-to-day business of the kingdom, and he soon ceased attending the meetings of the Council, or Cabinet, as it came to be called.

The English showed no more enthusiasm for their new monarch than he felt for them. They saw him as a foreigner, vaguely related to the Stuarts, but only brought in as a figure-head in order to keep a Roman Catholic out. George himself had a fund of homely common sense, but none of the grace and majesty that might have made him popular. Instead, he had the reputation of hating his own eldest son, of having divorced his wife and shut her up in a castle for life, and he was accompanied to England by a pair of extraordinarily ugly women, one so thin that she was nicknamed " the Maypole ", and the other so fat that she was known as " the Elephant ".

36

GEORGE I

" THE FIFTEEN "

George I knew that he owed his throne to the Whigs and he naturally chose them for his ministers. The leaders were General Stanhope (who had captured Minorca in 1708), Sunderland, Lord Townshend and his brother-in-law, Robert Walpole.

Almost at once the new government had to face a Jacobite rising. Stuart hopes had always rested upon military help from France and organised support in Britain, but since there was little prospect of either, the 1715 Rebellion was a failure from the start.

By the Treaty of Utrecht, old Louis XIV had promised not to help the Pretender. But, as long as Louis was alive, the Jacobites could hope, since everyone knew that he would break a promise if it suited him. However, Louis died in 1715 and French policy changed. The new king, Louis XV, was a child, and the Regent of France, Philip of Orleans, knew that Philip V of Spain (the little boy's uncle) could claim the French throne. Therefore he decided to avoid trouble with England.

Undismayed by this lack of French support, Jacobite plans went forward. In Scotland, where the Union was still far from popular, the Earl of Mar had been disappointed at failing to secure a worthwhile post from the English Whigs. He declared for the Jacobite cause and called out the clans. Mar, known as " Bobbing John " from the way in which he changed from one political side to the other, soon had a sizeable force of Highlanders at Perth. Had he been anything of a leader, he could easily have advanced to Edinburgh.

The Jacobite Rebellion 1715

In London, Stanhope and Townshend acted promptly. Some leading Jacobites were arrested, Admiral Byng was despatched to keep watch on the French coast, Argyll collected the Campbells to deal with Mar, while the main body of troops in England stood by to suppress any uprising.

A small force of Jacobites in the north-east of England moved along the Border to link up with some Lowlanders and a few clansmen sent by Mar. Four or five thousand men entered Lancashire but were easily scattered by Stanhope's commanders. Meanwhile, Argyll and Mar met at *Sherriffmuir* in Perthshire (November 13th, 1715), where in a half-hearted engagement,

> " We ran and they ran, and they ran and we ran,
>   And we ran and they ran awa', man ! "

Mar withdrew to Perth, thereby making certain of failure, since the Highlanders could only be held together by swift victories. At the end of December, the Pretender himself, James Edward Stuart (" James III "), landed in Scotland. He was too late, and his glum manner was not likely to put new heart into his supporters. As Mar's army dwindled, Argyll's force was strengthened by Dutch and Swiss troops.

But there was no more fighting. In February, Mar and the melancholy Pretender took ship for France and the " Fifteen " petered out. James Edward Stuart went to Avignon where he dismissed Bolingbroke, the one able man in his service, and later he moved his Court to Italy.

The Rebellion made the Government realise the dangers of having no friends in Europe, especially when there were strong rumours that Sweden was going to take the place of France as friend of the Jacobites. Moreover, as Elector of Hanover, George I was deeply concerned for the safety of his beloved

THE CLANS
WERE CALLED OUT

little country while there was war between Sweden and Peter the Great of Russia.

Stanhope therefore went to work to find allies. To everyone's astonishment, he managed to form the Triple Alliance between Britain, Holland and France. In 1718 this became the Quadruple Alliance when Austria joined the others. These strangely assorted partners had come together to support each other's interests. Both France and Austria wanted a check put on the ambitions of Philip of Spain, so Admiral Byng obligingly sailed to the Mediterranean and destroyed the Spanish fleet at *Cape Passaro*. Another British fleet went to the Baltic to secure a couple of ports which George I wanted to round off the territory of Hanover. Largely as a result of these manoeuvres, Spain was checked and Sweden quickly went into decline, so that Russia became the chief Power in the Baltic. This was by no means to George I's liking, but there was little he could do about it, and Britain was soon to withdraw from European affairs for a period of twenty years.

PROPOSING A TOAST

THE SOUTH SEA BUBBLE, 1720

During these events, George I went off to Hanover, as he did whenever possible, taking Stanhope with him. The Prince of Wales, afterwards George II, took charge at home with Townshend and Walpole as his chief advisers. Sunderland soon stirred up trouble by suggesting to the King that these three were making themselves popular behind his back and were planning to set up a party of their own.

Like most of the Hanoverians, George I thoroughly disliked his eldest son. Mere suspicion was enough to make him dismiss Townshend, whereupon Walpole resigned in sympathy. By good fortune, therefore, Walpole happened to be out of office when the South

Walpole luckily out of office

Sea Bubble burst, bringing disgrace upon all who were in the Government.

A scheme to make fortunes

The South Sea Company had been formed in 1711 to trade with the Spanish colonies in South and Central America. It had not done particularly well until the Directors hit upon a plan to make their fortunes. They offered to take over the National Debt, so that people who had lent money to the Government became shareholders in the Company. Moreover, the Company offered to pay the Government seven million pounds for this privilege. At once the public thought that the Company's trading prospects must be enormously valuable and they rushed forward to buy its shares. The whole scheme appeared to be absolutely respectable since ministers were taking part, and the shares shot up from £100 to £300 in a week; by the summer of 1720, the price had risen to £1000 a share.

Share-buying became a mania. Rumours of rich opportunities and discoveries urged the public on; Walpole raised a warning voice, but no one listened as the boom reached its peak. New companies were formed on every side for such projects as making a wheel of perpetual motion, obtaining gold from sea-water, importing jackasses to breed mules and others as absurd as they were dishonest.

When some of these companies were shown up as frauds, people began to wonder about their own wisdom. Everyone decided to sell. Share prices collapsed, and men who had thought themselves

SHARE-BUYING BECAME A MANIA

wealthy one day found themselves ruined the next. HOGARTH'S PICTURE OF A BUSY SCENE OUTSIDE THE CUSTOMS HOUSE IN LONDON Some who had borrowed heavily to buy shares now found that they could not pay their debts ; some had to sell their estates and others, it was said, disappeared, went mad or committed suicide.

Anger followed panic. Furious blame was laid on the Government and accusations of fraud were hurled at ministers, officials and even at the King, since it was known that his mistresses had taken part in the gamble. It seemed certain that the Whigs would be ruined. Tory hopes and Jacobite dreams began to revive, but the man who came to the rescue was the Whig who had warned people from the start about the danger of gambling in shares.

Sir Robert Walpole was not a member of the Government when the Bubble burst, so it was felt that his hands were sufficiently clean to tidy up the mess. He already had a reputation for his understanding of money matters and, by skilful management, he cut down the losses and saved the Whig party from disaster.

41

SIR ROBERT
WALPOLE

Thus, in 1721, Walpole became undisputed leader of the country. He held the offices of First Lord of the Treasury and Chancellor of the Exchequer, with Townshend and Carteret, a young man of promise, as his two secretaries of state. In fact, though not in name, Walpole was the first Prime Minister.

"LET SLEEPING DOGS LIE"

Robert Walpole was a wealthy squire with an estate at Houghton in Norfolk. Stout, red-faced and jovial, fond of company, of eating, drinking and coarse jokes, he was in many ways typical of the landed class that ruled the countryside. It was said that he started the Saturday holiday for Parliament so that he could go hunting, and it was well known that he always opened his Norfolk bailiff's letters to read the news about crops and neighbours before turning his attention to the affairs of state.

THE COUNTRY
HOUSEWIFE

As a Whig, a farmer and astute businessman, Walpole's policy was to make the country prosperous and to keep everything quiet and comfortable. Discontent could bring back the Stuarts, so Walpole cultivated peace and trade. Because he steered clear of trouble for twenty years, his policy was summed up in a Latin phrase, "Quieta non movere", which can be translated into the English saying, "Let sleeping dogs lie".

There were many stories that Walpole kept his power by bribery—"the bottomless pocket of Robin" was often mentioned when his opponents accused him of rewarding his friends and supporters. The bluff, cunning squire certainly saw nothing wrong in using every means to keep himself in power. There were many positions at Court and in the Government service which carried large salaries for doing next to nothing, and Walpole saw to it that these comfortable

jobs, known as " sinecures ", went to men who supported him.

He had a low opinion of human nature, believing
that men acted, not from a sense of duty, but for gain.
" All these men have their price ", he once remarked
contemptuously about some of his opponents, and
though he himself was not dishonest, he was clever
enough to make a fortune. He spent hugely, and
lavished £100,000 on rebuilding and refurnishing his
home in Norfolk, though his son Horace afterwards
described it, most unfairly, as " neither magnificent
nor beautiful, there is great expense without either
judgement or taste ".

His policy of letting sleeping dogs lie can be seen in
the way Walpole tackled the country's business. He
reduced taxes, kept the land-tax very low to avoid
upsetting the landed gentry and encouraged trade by
helping manufacturers to import raw materials and
to export their finished goods. Customs duties were
lowered and the colonies were assisted, though they
were not expected to trade with anyone else except the
home country.

Smuggling at this time amounted almost to an
industry, so the powers of the Revenue officers were
increased and certain goods, such as tea, coffee and
cocoa, had to be placed in special or " bonded "
warehouses. When these goods were taken from the
warehouses to be sold to the public, a duty had to be
paid known as " excise ". This system of bonded
warehousing was a severe blow at the smugglers and it
increased the Government's income.

Walpole introduced his *Excise Bill* to include
wines and tobacco in the same system, but he soon
found that he had aroused a hornet's nest. A tremendous outcry arose at the prospect of Revenue officers

SMUGGLERS

PORTEOUS
DRAGGED TO
THE GALLOWS

prying into Englishmen's homes, so, although he reckoned that the gains would be great, Walpole gave way and let the matter drop.

The celebrated cases of *Wood's Halfpence* (1724) and the *Porteous Riots* (1736) are two more examples of Walpole's policy of letting sleeping dogs lie, though here he was soothing them back to sleep after they had awoken in anger. A man named Wood had bought the right to supply Ireland with copper coins when it was discovered that he intended to cheat the Irish by supplying coins of less than face-value. Dean Swift, author of *Gulliver's Travels*, attacked the swindle in *The Drapier's Letters*, so Walpole calmed the storm by withdrawing Wood's monopoly. Quietly, he saw to it that Wood was given pension as compensation !

Some years later, a Captain Porteous ordered the Edinburgh Town Guard to open fire on a mob which was trying to rescue a popular smuggler. Several persons were killed, for which the unfortunate Porteous was condemned to death. Queen Caroline, acting as Regent in the absence of George II, ordered his reprieve, whereupon the mob dragged Porteous from prison and hanged him. The Queen wanted severe punishment laid on the city, but Walpole saw the danger of trouble in Scotland, where the Porteous Riots might flare up into a Jacobite rising, so he persuaded the Queen to do nothing worse than award a pension to the Captain's widow.

The Porteous Riots

44

THE FALL OF WALPOLE

So fond of power was Walpole that he kept control of everything and everyone. Carteret resigned in disgust as early as 1724 and, although foreign affairs were at first left to Townshend, Walpole quarrelled with his brother-in-law, who quitted politics in 1730 to devote himself to farming with such success that he won the famous nickname of "Turnip" Townshend.

When George I died in 1727 it seemed as if the Norfolk squire's reign had also come to an end. It was known that the new King had called him "a rogue and a rascal" and that he favoured Sir Spencer Compton, Speaker of the House. But poor Compton was so ill-fitted for the post of chief minister that he even had to turn to Walpole for help in preparing the King's Speech. Meanwhile, the old fox had played his cards well. He realised that Caroline was the real ruler of her pompous, fussy little husband, and he had long since won her regard. Caroline's private life was far from happy ; she quarrelled with her eldest son* and was constantly irritated by her husband's exasperating ways and unfaithfulness, but she was an intelligent and courageous woman. She soon convinced George that his kingdom could not possibly manage without the redoubtable Walpole, and the astute minister was soon more firmly in the saddle than ever.

Death of George I

A SAILOR WITH
A BOATHOOK

Even so, an Opposition formed against Walpole. William Pulteney and some of the younger men in Parliament, notably Henry Fox and William Pitt (at this time a Cornet, or junior officer, in the Dragoon

* Frederick, Prince of Wales, was one of the most unpleasant and unpopular princes in history. His own mother, Queen Caroline, once said of him, " My dear first-born is the greatest ass, and the greatest liar . . . and the greatest beast in the whole world, and I heartily wish he were out of it ".

Guards), ceaselessly attacked what they called the " Robinocracy "—the one-man rule of " Robin " Walpole. Acting partly from envy and partly from the feeling that their talents were neglected, the Opposition called themselves " The Patriots ", though Walpole jeeringly referred to them as " the boys ", and gathered around Frederick, Prince of Wales, who was detested by his parents even more than George II had been disliked by his own father. When they took up the Prince of Wales's claim for a higher allowance, the King was so furious that Pitt lost his cornetcy.

A quarrel with Spain

But it was a foreign war and not home affairs that brought Walpole down. He had long managed to keep England clear of all continental entanglements, including the War of the Polish Succession (1733–38), but it was a trading squabble with Spain which led, first, to a trivial war, and then to a world-wide struggle.

By the *Assiento*, a clause in the Treaty of Utrecht, Britain had the right to sell 4800 slaves a year to the Spanish colonies in South America and also to send one shipload of merchandise for trading. English merchants used this agreement to carry on a large amount of illegal trade, and the Spaniards insisted on their right to search British ships which they suspected. The British denied this right and complained that peaceful merchantmen were being treated with violence.

The Opposition made the most of this situation, insisting that Walpole's weak-kneed policy was humiliating Britain and harming her trade. They brought into the House of Commons a certain Captain Jenkins who produced from a box an ear which, he said, had been cut from his own head by Spanish officials who had boarded his ship.

This absurd incident caught the public's imagination, and a wave of anger swept the country into war with Spain. Walpole ridiculed his aggressive

CAPTAIN JENKINS AT THE
HOUSE OF COMMONS

countrymen who rejoiced as if a great victory had already been won : " They are ringing the bells now," he grimly remarked, " but they soon will be wringing their hands."

Walpole believed that France would side with Spain and that this must lead to a long and costly war. He was quite right, but where he himself had failed was in not having prepared to defend the prosperity that his peaceful policy had created.

In the war with Spain there were a few small successes at sea, but years of economy had reduced the Navy to a pitiful state, so that next to nothing was achieved by a navy and by troops whose morale and equipment were in very poor shape.

During the war, Commodore George Anson was despatched with six ships " to vex the Spaniards " on a voyage round the Horn into the Pacific. He captured some prizes, but the slight damage to the Spaniards was nothing compared with the magnificent example of his voyage round the world. Despite storms and scurvy, Anson's seamanship, discoveries and leadership provided inspiration for his young officers and hard-bitten seamen.

Anson's Voyage 1740–44

Nothing of this was known at home, where the Opposition, having goaded Walpole into war, now attacked him for not winning it. A general election so reduced his supporters that in 1741, the old minister retired into private life as the Earl of Orford. His twenty years of peace and security had provided Britain with reserves of wealth to stand the strain of two major wars, but, for the moment, she was friendless and ill-prepared.

Walpole retires

CHAPTER 4

GREAT BRITAIN WINS AN EMPIRE

THE removal of Captain Jenkins' celebrated ear caused an outburst of bad temper that led to war with Spain, and then to a struggle with France for sea-power and for the colonies that depended upon sea-power.

At the time, few people grasped that this was the real object of the war. Even statesmen looked upon the colonies as trading-stations which provided pleasant luxuries in peace-time, but which were likely to prove expensive handicaps during a war.

By now, France no longer felt it necessary to keep on good terms with Britain, and she had made the " Family Compact " with Spain, agreeing that together they would recover Gibraltar and Minorca. Far away, in North America and India, rivalry between French and British settlers was becoming so heated that little excuse would be needed to bring about an armed struggle. Nearer home, the increasing bad feeling between the two countries was causing the Jacobites to raise their glasses to toast the prospect of a Stuart king at Westminster.

In northern Europe a small country lying next to Hanover, with poor soil and barely two million inhabitants, had suddenly become dangerously important. Frederick William I, King of Prussia, a ruler " with the mind of a drill-sergeant, the manners of

a boor and the moods of a savage ", had turned his sturdy, obedient people into a race of soldiers. His son, Frederick II, afterwards called Frederick the Great, inherited the best army in Europe and began to make its existence known. This young man, cultured, literary and musical, had not yet shown that his talents concealed a ruthless mind and a genius for war.

The situation was explosive ; Britain, cocksure and prosperous, was already at fisticuffs with Spain ; France was ready to join in to help her ally, her colonists and the Jacobites ; Frederick of Prussia was itching to use his magnificent army. The opportunity for them all arrived at the moment when Charles VI of Austria died.

The Emperor Charles had two daughters but no son. Anxious that the Austrian Empire should remain in his family, Charles devoted his last years to arranging that his daughter Maria Theresa should inherit his possessions. He issued a solemn decree, known as a *Pragmatic Sanction*, and persuaded the leading nations of Europe, including Britain, to accept it.

A CAVALRY
OFFICER WEARING
A WIG

In 1740 Charles VI died, and Maria Theresa succeeded to Austria's great possessions. Frederick of Prussia announced his support for her, and then, almost immediately, seized *Silesia*, one of her richest provinces. As soon as Frederick behaved like a scoundrel, there were others to follow his example. France, Spain and Bavaria found excuses to join Prussia, while Britain (and therefore Hanover), Holland and little Savoy, supported Maria Theresa.

THE WAR OF THE AUSTRIAN SUCCESSION, 1740–1748

The war that broke out between these Powers was a confused affair, in which each sought his own advantage and some, like Britain and France, were not officially at war for years. George II's concern for Hanover meant that Britain became involved in continental campaigns without much success, whereas being a naval power, her real interests lay on the seas.

A confused war

Walpole's successor was Henry Pelham, but foreign

ENG. BK. III—4

*George II in
action*

affairs were in the hands of Carteret, who infused
some life into the conduct of the war. He increased
the financial aid (subsidy) to Maria Theresa and sent
a combined army of British and Hanoverian soldiers
to Germany, where George II, leading his troops,
sword in hand, and roaring, " Steady, my brave
boys, steady ! " won the *Battle of Dettingen* (1745)
against the French.

Carteret's aim was to patch up the quarrel between
Austria and Prussia, in order to concentrate against
France. But though he had ability, Carteret mis-
managed the war and treated his colleagues so
arrogantly that he fell from office. Pelham and his
brother, the Duke of Newcastle, carried on the

government with various Whigs, but not with William Pitt, whose sarcastic gibes at Hanover, " the beggarly Electorate ", had mortally offended George II.

The French assembled an army at Dunkirk under the great Marshal Saxe. Then, after a gale had scattered the invasion fleet, Saxe moved into the Netherlands and defeated the Anglo-Hanoverian army under the Duke of Cumberland (George II's son) at *Fontenoy*, where the British regiments fought with stubborn courage.

A FOOT SOLDIER

" THE FORTY-FIVE "

War between England and France naturally caused a fever of hopeful excitement among the Jacobites. All their hopes rested upon Charles Edward Stuart, the twenty-five-year-old son of the Old Pretender. The French fleet, however, was scattered, and Saxe was fully occupied in the Netherlands, but Charles Edward was brave, determined and young.

In July 1745 the Young Pretender landed on the West coast of Scotland, with only seven friends. His second ship, laden with the arms, money and ammunition that he had manfully scraped together, had been intercepted and driven back to France. At first the prince met with a cool reception from the chieftains, but affection and loyalty to the Stuarts still lingered in the Highlands. The clansmen, who recognised in their minds the rashness of rebellion, surrendered their hearts to the appeal of the handsome, gallant youth. They said he was doomed, but if he marched, they would follow. In August the Stuart standard was raised in the presence of about a thousand Highlanders, few enough to conquer a kingdom.

" Bonnie Prince Charlie " lands in Scotland

The Government in England had been warned of

the venture, but had made no preparations. George II was in Hanover and the army in Flanders, and though both were hastily brought back, the only force to oppose Charles Edward for the moment was a small body of regulars under Sir John Cope. Easily avoiding him, the Young Pretender marched to Perth, where he proclaimed his father James VIII, and proceeded to Edinburgh, which he entered on 16th September. Cope's force approached the city but was put to flight in ten minutes at *Prestonpans*.

For six weeks Charles remained at Holyrood, winning the hearts of everyone, especially the ladies, but waiting in vain for word of a general uprising in his favour. The interval was fatal, for it gave the Government time to bring back Cumberland and his army, and for old General Wade to reach Newcastle with a strong force.

On November 3rd the march on England began. Wade's army was avoided, for Charles took the westward route, captured Carlisle and entered Lancashire with about 5000 Highlanders. But the English Jacobites sat tight. Enthusiasm for the Stuarts had been cooling for 30 years, the cause was tainted with Catholic and French support, and there was too little prospect of success to encourage men to risk their lives and fortunes. The Whig government might be in a bad way and the Hanoverians unloved, but Walpole's long reign had done its work. Rebellion could not prosper in a comfortable land.

BONNIE PRINCE CHARLIE
AT HOLYROOD

ON " BLACK FRIDAY " THE SCOTS BEGAN THE LONG MARCH BACK

On December 4th Charles Edward reached Derby,
130 miles from London, and here the chieftains
refused to march another step. Their reasons were
sound. Wade and Cumberland were behind them
with larger armies ; they were cut off from their base,
with no sign of support on any side : if they went back
Scotland might be secured, but if they went on, the
Jacobite cause was ruined. They could not know
that London was guarded only by a camp at Finchley,
that the capital was in a panic, with the Bank of
England paying out in sixpences to gain time. Charles
was a gambler and his luck might have held. One
charge by the Highlanders could have swept him
past the apprentice boys and into the heart of London.
After that, anything might have happened. Retreat
made failure certain and it broke Charles Edward's *Retreat from*
heart. *Derby*

On " Black Friday " the Scots turned their faces
north and began the long march back, with Cumberland on their heels. Lord George Murray held up
the pursuit and, on December 26th, the Prince reached
Glasgow, where he gained some reinforcements. A
victory at *Falkirk* over Hawley, Wade's successor, was
the last success, for Cumberland came on steadily into

53

Inverness · Culloden 1746

Moidart · Dalwhinnie
Dunkeld
Perth
Stirling
Glasgow · Edinburgh
Falkirk · Prestonpans
1746
· Kelso

Carlisle
Penrith
Kendal
Lancaster
Preston
Wigan · Manchester
Macclesfield
Cheadle · Derby

0   50   100
Miles

– · – · – Route followed by Prince
Charles from the landing at Moidart
to the Battle of Culloden

the Highlands, with a well-equipped army, supported by a naval force that moved along the coast. On April 17th, 1746, the Jacobite cause was crushed at *Culloden Moor*. After the battle, " Butcher " Cumberland reduced the Highlands with savage thoroughness that tarnished his name for ever. The courage of the Highlanders deserved a soldier's respect, but it was punished by the slaughter of clansmen and the burning of their pitiable crofts.

With a price on his head of £30,000, the Young Pretender wandered about the Highlands and among the Islands for five months. The tales of his escapes and of the noble loyalty of penniless Highlanders have cast a romantic glow upon a venture that was doomed from the outset. At last Charles Edward reached France, more than a year after he had set out in high hopes.

CHARLES EDWARD LEAVES FOR FRANCE

He left behind an immortal legend, but he never saw
Scotland again, and when he died in 1788, a weary *Pitt in office*
old drunkard, the cause of the White Cockade had
long been dead.

THE TREATY OF AIX-LA-CHAPELLE

The '45 Rebellion brought William Pitt into the
government.   The Pelhams felt that he could
strengthen their weak position, but George II refused
to entertain the idea of promoting a man who had
insulted Hanover. The government then resigned,
and for the first time, a King was forced to accept a
minister of whom he disapproved.   Pitt became
Paymaster of the Forces, and for the next ten years
remained in this unimportant post from which he
was to step into power and fame.

The War of the Austrian Succession dragged on its
confused way for two more years.   Prussia, having
come to terms with Maria Theresa, had withdrawn
from the fighting, Philip V of Spain died and his son
put an end to the Italian campaign, but Marshal
Saxe conquered almost all the Austrian Netherlands,
where Cumberland had returned to lead the Anglo-
Hanoverian army with more courage than skill.

At sea, however, the British Navy had somewhat
recovered from its low condition. In 1747 Anson
and Warren defeated the French off *Cape Finisterre* ;
Hawke broke up another fleet near *Belle Île* off the
coast of Brittany.

In North America, *Louisbourg*, the great French
fortress guarding the Gulf of Lawrence, had been
captured in 1745, but this was offset by the loss of
Madras in India, where Governor Dupleix was
energetically advancing the interests of France.

The war ground to an end in 1748, but the Treaty
of Aix-la-Chapelle solved nothing. Prussia kept

Silesia, Louisbourg was exchanged for Madras, and poor Maria Theresa gained nothing and lost a great deal. The quarrels between Prussia and Austria and between France and Britain had not been settled, and the next seven years were no more than a truce.

THE PERIOD OF TRUCE, 1748–1755

A truce in Europe did not change the situation in North America and India, where English and French settlers stood face to face with unconcealed enmity, and where the Treaty of Aix-la-Chapelle meant little to men who were defending their farms or the trade of their Company.

Rivals in North America

In North America the English colonies lay along the eastern seaboard, whereas the French possessions were along the St. Lawrence River, around the Great Lakes, and down the Mississippi. Two areas, in particular, were hotly disputed : *Acadia* (Nova Scotia), and the *Ohio Valley*, which provided a link between French Canada and the Mississippi settlements. If this valley became French, it would prove a barrier to British expansion westwards. Thus, whether there was peace in Europe or not, raids and counter-raids took place in these areas, where both sides sought the help of Red Indian allies.

Though the French were outnumbered by twenty to one, they were better organised and more mobile than the British settlers, for as trappers, fur-traders and foresters, the tough, wary Frenchmen earned the respect of the Indians, with whom they usually traded fairly. After the " peace " of 1748 both sides prepared for war. Louisbourg was strengthened and the French also began building a line of forts (Niagara, Crown Point, Frontenac, Ticonderoga, and Duquesne) to link up Canada with Louisana in the south.

The first serious clash occurred in 1754 when a

The map contains the following labels:

North America in the 18th Century

Hudson Bay
NEWFOUNDLAND
R St Lawrence
Cape Breton Is.
Louisburg X
NEW BRUNSWICK
ACADIA
NOVA SCOTIA
Halifax
Quebec X
Montreal
Crown Point
Ft. Ticonderoga
Concord
L. Superior
L. Huron
Ft. Frontenac
L. Michigan
L. Ontario
Saratoga
Ft. Oswego
Ft. Niagara
NEW ENGLAND
Boston (M)
L. Erie
New York
PENNSYLVANIA
Philadelphia
Ft. Duquesne
Brandywine
Long Island
R. Missouri
R. Mississippi
MARYLAND
VIRGINIA
R. Ohio
Allegheny Mountains
Yorktown
NORTH CAROLINA
SOUTH CAROLINA
Charleston
R. Mississippi
LOUISIANA
Savannah
GEORGIA
FLORIDA
Gulf of Mexico

0 200 400

Areas of French settlement to 1763

Boundary of the 13 Colonies which became the original U.S.A

(M) Massachusetts

Concord
Lexington
Bunker's Hill
Boston
Boston Bay

detachment under young Colonel Washington over-
powered a French force advancing from Fort
Duquesne, though this defeat was soon avenged by a
larger expedition that forced Washington to surrender.
A year later, General Braddock, who had been sent out
from England, was ambushed in the woods near Fort   *A defeat in*
Duquesne by a force of French and Indians who   *America*
wiped out nearly all the regular soldiers. Meanwhile,
Admiral Boscawen, endeavouring to prevent the
arrival of 3000 French troops in Canada, captured

FRENCH AND INDIANS AMBUSH BRADDOCK'S REGULARS

two warships off Newfoundland. Yet, so far, war had not been officially declared.

In the West Indies, where Britain, France and Spain all had valuable possessions, there was a similar state of tension. Warships patrolled the seas, partly to cope with the pirates and partly to keep an eye on their rivals ; garrisons of fever-stricken soldiers were kept at the ready, since hostilities in Europe always led to attacks and counter-attacks between the islands.

INDIA

In India, Portugal and Holland had small possessions, but the chief rivals were the East India Companies of France and Britain.

French and English trading companies

Along the south-east coast, known as the *Carnatic*, the French headquarters were at Pondicherry, and there were also some " factories ", or trading-posts, such as Hugle, in Bengal far to the north. On the west coast, the chief French trading-stations were Calicut, Surat and Mahé.

The English Company had three main stations

("presidencies")—Bombay on the west coast, Calcutta (Fort William) in Bengal, and Madras (Fort St. George) in the Carnatic. Each of the presidencies had several "factories" under its control.

Both companies had originally come to India to trade, and had obtained concessions from the local rulers to build warehouses with forts to protect their goods. India, however, was in a state of chaos, for the rule of the Great Mogul had broken down, and nawabs and rajahs were struggling for independence, for survival or for conquest. In this situation, a determined and wily governor, with a few well-armed European soldiers, could meddle in local politics to improve the position of his Company.

Dupleix, the French governor of Pondicherry since 1741, was just such a man. Far-sighted and clever, aided by a good commander and a fine admiral, Dupleix was working on his great scheme to bring the Carnatic, and then the whole of the south (the Deccan) under French control. By supporting pretenders and claimants, Dupleix was able to set up puppet-rulers who depended for their power upon his assistance. When the English awoke to the danger, Dupleix was well on the way to becoming master of Southern

Governor-general Dupleix

India. Indeed, if the French Government had given him even reasonable support, he must have succeeded.

In 1750 Dupleix was assisting a claimant to the throne of the Carnatic, whose rightful ruler, Mohammed Ali, was hotly besieged in *Trichinopoly*. If that fortress fell, the Carnatic would come under French control and British trade there would be doomed.

INDIA IN CLIVE'S TIME

At this point Robert Clive, formerly a clerk but
now an officer in the Company's forces, obtained
permission to seize Arcot, the local capital, which had
been left undefended during the siege of Trichinopoly.
With a handful of European troops and 600 Indian
soldiers (sepoys) Clive easily captured *Arcot*, but then
had to hold its crumbling walls for 50 days against an
army of 10,000 that marched from Trichinopoly.
This famous siege changed the situation, for Clive
not only restored the prestige of the English, but
afterwards was able to defeat the French candidate,
and to restore Mohammed Ali to his throne. Dupleix
strove to win back his influence, but in 1754 he was
recalled to France in disgrace, not so much for waging
war without permission as for failing to win it.

Thus, by the narrowest of margins, English trade
in India had been saved, and Clive, no longer the
wild scalliwag whose parents had gratefully packed
him off to the East, came home in 1755 to enjoy the
fortune that his successes had brought.

THE SEVEN YEARS WAR, 1756–1763

We have seen that the Treaty of Aix-la-Chapelle
settled nothing, and that the interval between 1748
and 1756 was merely a truce disregarded in India
and America. When the war re-opened, there was a
startling change of partners.

CLIVE AT ARCOT

The Austrian Chancellor, Kaunitz, knew that the real enemy was Prussia, and he pointed out to Louis XV that the sole winner in the late war had been Frederick the Great. It was surely absurd for France and Austria, both Catholic powers, to fight each other to a standstill merely to benefit Prussia, an upstart Protestant state.

Frederick foresaw this situation, and since he was also on bad terms with Russia because of his insulting remarks about the Tsarina Elizabeth, he looked round for an ally. He knew that George II would prefer a friend to an enemy on the borders of his beloved Hanover, so it was not difficult for Britain and Prussia to reach an agreement.

ROBERT CLIVE

Thus, in the Seven Years War, France and Austria, soon joined by Russia, took sides against Britain and Prussia.

Though war had long been in the air, Britain was as ill-prepared as usual. When Henry Pelham had died in 1754 old George II had remarked, correctly, " Now, I shall have no more peace ", for Pelham's brother, the scheming Duke of Newcastle, became chief minister. Expert in controlling the House of Commons by means of his wealth and the " pocket boroughs ", Newcastle was no statesman, and the army and navy were once again in wretched condition to fight a major war.

In April 1756 the French pounced on *Minorca*. Admiral Sir John Byng was sent to recapture the island, but after a brush with the enemy fleet, in which *Loss of Minorca* he did not engage his main force, Byng withdrew to Gibraltar. He felt that he was not strong enough to defeat the French, but might well lose Gibraltar as well.

Byng's fleet was certainly not a powerful one, but almost any other English admiral would have fought. The public, always furious at humiliation on the sea,

clamoured for the culprit, and Byng was brought home
under arrest, court-martialled and shot for cowardice.
It was a harsh, and somewhat unfair, sentence. The
French writer Voltaire acidly remarked that the
English shot their admirals " to encourage the
others ", but, in fact, the execution of Byng did remind
sea-commanders that it was better to take bold risks
than to fail through caution.

The loss of Minorca was followed by news that
Montcalm, the brilliant French commander in
Canada, had captured Fort *Oswego*, and that a British
attack on Louisbourg had failed. In Europe
Frederick the Great had marched into Saxony, but
though this gave him a temporary advantage, he was
soon surrounded by his enemies, and defeated at
Kolin (June 1758). At *Rochefort*, on the French
coast, a strong British attack was beaten off, and in
Germany, the Duke of Cumberland was trapped and
forced to surrender at *Klosterseven* (1757), where he had
to agree to the occupation of Hanover by French
troops. Poor George II cried out, " Here is my son
who has ruined me and disgraced himself ". It seemed
as if Britain was about to be overthrown in Europe, in
Canada and in India.*

GEORGE II

* Clive had returned to India where the Nawab of Bengal captured
Fort William and imprisoned 146 captives in the " Black Hole of

Only disaster could have brought William Pitt into office and to the rescue. Newcastle, who had faced the news of defeats by feebly moaning, " We are not singly a match for France ", gave up control of the government and Pitt became Secretary of State.

For years Pitt had attacked Newcastle with biting sarcasm. He was popular and the country shared his opinion of himself—" I know that I can save this country," he declared, " and no one else can "—but in Parliament his position was weak, for Newcastle pulled all the strings. As for George II, he could scarcely bear to set eyes on Pitt, " the terrible cornet of horse ", who had been so rude about him, his ministers and his homeland.

" I know that I can save this country "

No sooner in, than the King found an excuse to dismiss Pitt, but it was then found impossible to form a government without him. The public showed their indignation at his dismissal by awarding him the Freedom of nineteen of the chief towns, and they dubbed him " The Great Commoner " for his defiance of King, prince and aristocracy.

A solution had to be found. It was a shabby one, but it served. Newcastle could not run the government without Pitt, and Pitt knew that he could not win the war while Newcastle could manipulate Parliament like a puppet-theatre. So they agreed to work together, Pitt to manage the war and Newcastle to carry on the backstairs management he loved so well.

" THE GREAT COMMONER "

King George was persuaded to agree. " Sir," said Pitt to the testy old King, " give me your confidence and I will deserve it," to which George II growled,

---

Calcutta ". Clive and Admiral Watson soon defeated the Nawab and made him sign a treaty. In June 1757 Clive won the Battle of Plassey and brought Bengal under British rule, but the news of this victory was not known in England for a considerable time.

" Deserve my confidence and you shall have it." To the end, neither failed to keep his bargain.

Pitt the leader

As in 1940, disaster brought to power a great man who had long been in the background, warning Britain of danger and proclaiming his own ability to rescue the country. Like Winston Churchill, Pitt was a matchless orator and a commanding figure whose mere glance could wither an opponent into silence. Not only could Pitt see the war as a whole, to be fought out on distant fields and oceans, but he also had the gift of choosing the right men to command. At a time when it was infinitely more difficult for a politician to speak to the country than in our day, Pitt was able to convince people that he kept nothing back but relied upon their courage and support for victory. Above all, he had the true leader's power to inspire men. " No man," it was said, " ever entered his closet who did not feel himself braver at his return than when he went in."

Pitt's policy was to strike hard and often at France so that she would never know where the next blow might fall. He had formerly opposed the help that was given to foreign allies, but now he realised that Frederick the Great must be supported at all costs.

Support for Prussia

Gold was poured out to keep the Prussian soldiers in the field under their remorseless commander. The Anglo-Hanoverian army was strengthened to ward off the French while Frederick grappled with the huge armies of Russia and Austria.

Attacks were made up and down the French coast, not with any major successes, but they tied up French forces which otherwise would have been used against the Prussians. The British Navy was kept at full stretch to prevent reinforcements reaching Canada, to support operations in the Baltic, the West Indies and off the coasts of West Africa and India. Pitt was waging world war. For this he appointed officers

of his own choice, soldiers like Amherst and Wolfe, *New commanders*
sailors like Boscawen and Keppel. The Duke of
Cumberland was replaced by Prince Ferdinand of
Brunswick, a brilliant soldier, who took over command
of the " Army of Observation " in Hanover.

In November 1757 Frederick of Prussia won a great
victory over the French at *Rossbach*, and, a month
later, another against the Austrians at *Leuthen*. News
of Clive's victory at *Plassey* put new heart into Britain,
which only a short time earlier, Pitt himself had
dubbed " this distressed and disgraced country ".

1758 began well. In Germany, Brunswick defeated
the French at *Crefeld* and drove them out of Hanover.
Across the Atlantic, General Amherst and Admiral
Boscawen captured Louisbourg, while, inland, forts
Frontenac, Oswego and Duquesne (renamed Fort
Pitt and, later, Pittsburg) were retaken.

A DRUMMER-BOY

The " wonder year ", 1759, when Horace Walpole
complained that the church bells were wearing out
through so much joyous pealing, opened with the
capture of *Guadeloupe*, the French sugar island in the
West Indies. Then, after Frederick had been hard-
pressed by the Russians and Austrians, Prussia was
saved by Brunswick's brilliant victory over the French
at *Minden* (40 miles from Hanover), where six English
regiments fought so magnificently that they still
bear " Minden " on their colours.

The most famous victory of the year came in September, when General Wolfe aided by Admiral
Saunders, achieved the impossible by getting an army
at night up on the Plains of Abraham in front of
Quebec. In the battle that resulted in the capture of
the city and, later, of the whole of Canada, both *Canada won*
Montcalm and Wolfe were killed, one in the hour of
defeat and the other at the moment of victory.

Meanwhile, the French prepared to invade England.
Warships and a fleet of flat-bottomed boats to trans-

WOLFE GIVES
HIS LAST ORDERS

port an army were gathered along the coast, but Pitt, instead of hiring foreign troops, called on Englishmen to defend their own country. Rear-Admiral Rodney was sent to patrol the Channel, Hawke sailed to the Bay of Biscay, and Boscawen to the Mediterranean to watch Toulon.

In August, when a French fleet left Toulon, Boscawen caught it and destroyed or captured most of the ships off *Cape Lagos*. In November, a storm scattered Admiral Hawke's fleet, and allowed the French Admiral to slip out of Brest with 26 warships that were to escort the invasion troops across the Channel. But Hawke re-appeared swiftly to drive the French ships into *Quiberon Bay*, a rocky inlet where they seemed to be safe. Hawke knew what Pitt expected and, with a gale behind him, he sailed boldly in to destroy some of the French ships and to drive the others on to the rocks. Quiberon Bay was the most decisive victory since the Armada, for the remnants of the French navy were scattered in various ports from which they dared not emerge to face the English squadrons. During 1759 alone, apart from the ships sunk or damaged, the British added to their own Navy no fewer than 27 French ships of the line.

With the war situation improving everywhere, Pitt was able to send help to Clive, whom he much admired and called " the heaven-born general ". A subsidy was granted to the East India Company, several warships and regiments were sent out, which restored the situation after some temporary French successes. In 1760 Colonel Coote defeated the French at *Wandewash* and then captured Pondicherry. French power in India had come to its end.

Victory in India

66

THE END OF THE WAR

In October, 1760, fiery little George II died, and, *George III* since his eldest son, Frederick Prince of Wales, *becomes King* jocularly known as " poor Fred ",* had already died, his grandson, aged 23, became George III.

The new king showed, almost at once, his desire for peace. To Pitt's astonishment, George spoke of " this bloody and expensive war ", whereas Pitt had plans in hand to extend its operations. Discovering that France and Spain were about to renew their alliance, he proposed to declare war on Spain.

The Cabinet refused to agree. Finding no support, Pitt resigned, with these indignant words :

> " I was called by my Sovereign and the Voice of the People to assist the State when others had abdicated . . . That being so, no one can be surprised that I will go on no longer since my advice is not taken."

Newcastle openly rejoiced at Pitt's fall, and George III's former tutor, a Scotsman named Lord Bute, became Secretary of State. As Pitt had forecast, war with Spain broke out in 1762, but owing to his preparations, it was brief and successful. Havana in the West Indies and Manila in the Philippines were captured, though the French actually took St. John's Newfoundland. On the excuse of supporting Portugal, Bute cut down the subsidies to Frederick, who never forgot or forgave the betrayal. Newcastle, edged out by Bute and ignored by the king, discovered

GEORGE III

* The famous rhyme about Frederick, the unpopular Prince of Wales is as follows :
" Here lies poor Fred Who was alive and is dead. Had it been his father I had much rather ; Had it been his brother Still better than another ; Had it been his sister No one would have missed her ; Had it been the whole generation Still better for the nation ; But since 'tis only Fred who was alive and is dead There's no more to be said."

too late that his day was over, and he, too, resigned. Peace was now certain, even if Frederick's interests were entirely forgotten.

The peace treaty

The Treaty of Paris (1763) that ended the Seven Years War, was a triumph for Britain, though people felt that Pitt would have gained even more. From France, Britain received Canada, Nova Scotia, Cape Breton Island, Grenada, Dominica, Tobago, Senegal and Minorca. She restored Guadeloupe and granted five unarmed trading stations in India. From Spain, Florida was gained but Cuba and the Philippines were handed back. Frederick of Prussia kept Silesia, but fifteen years later he was to have his revenge for being left in the lurch by George III. This desertion of an ally, not for the first time, confirmed the impression in Europe that Britain, " perfidious Albion ", was willing to pay gold for others to fight her land battles, but that she would abandon her friends whenever it suited her.

Pitt, more contemptuous of lesser men than ever, went into the background, growling mightily about the terms of the peace. Too arrogant to hold a following in peace-time and too disgruntled to serve George III, he retired to his country home from which, plagued by gout that made his temper worse than usual, he only emerged occasionally. By accepting the title of Earl of Chatham he damaged his popularity, and although he was to become the prime minister again for a short while, his days of triumph were over. Sick in body and disillusioned with his feeble colleagues, he left them to carry on as best they might, until, in less than two years, he resigned in favour of the Duke of Grafton.

A GOUT STOOL

THE WILKES AFFAIR

Between the dismissal of Pitt and his brief return occurred the episode of John Wilkes, one of the most celebrated champions of liberty in our history. Wilkes himself was an unholy scoundrel, as well as being one of the ugliest and most immoral men of his day.

George III was twenty-three when he succeeded his grandfather. Unlike the first two Hanoverians, he had been brought up as an Englishman and could barely speak German, but his mother, Princess Augusta, contemptuous of Parliament's control of the sovereign, never ceased telling him, " George, be a *King*."

George III's first steps had been to promote his friend Bute and to press for peace. Pitt had resigned and Newcastle soon followed him. When peace was made, the Princess-Mother cried triumphantly, " Now my son is really King ! " But George still had difficulties. Parliament refused to have Bute, Pitt would not return, so the king appointed as his chief minister George Grenville, who did not oppose the use of places and pensions to create a party of " King's Friends " in Parliament.

It was at this stage that John Wilkes came to the fore. He had been elected Member of Parliament for Aylesbury, and, early in the reign, he started *The North Briton* to attack Bute and the Government. Number 45 of the journal was so violently sarcastic about the King's Speech that George III instructed Grenville to prosecute Wilkes for libel. He was arrested, but popular opinion in London was on his side. When he claimed freedom of speech as an M.P., the Chief Justice decided in his favour. Knowing that he would be arrested again when Parliament was dissolved, Wilkes went abroad and made himself notorious for his dissipated behaviour.

John Wilkes arrested

The Middlesex Election

In 1768, after Pitt had given way to Grafton, Wilkes returned and was promptly elected to Parliament for Middlesex, one of the few constituencies where popularity counted more than influence. The king, however, had not forgotten his impudence and made Grafton declare the election void. Amid frantic excitement and cries of " Wilkes and Liberty ", Wilkes was elected a second time and again the election was quashed. A third election produced the same result, but Wilkes's opponent, with only 296 votes to 1143 was declared elected.

Wilkes was arrested and sent to prison, but his popularity gained him election as an Alderman of the City of London, and eventually as Lord Mayor. In 1775, when the king decided to let " that devil Wilkes " alone, he returned to Parliament and became comparatively respectable in his old age.

The importance of this ferociously ugly spendthrift was that Wilkes stood for the liberty of electors to choose whom they pleased, for freedom to report debates in Parliament and for the rights of a subject against arrest by " general warrant " (in which no one was mentioned by name). The affair showed the Government that liberty was still precious even when its banner was carried by a scoundrel.

" WILKES AND LIBERTY "

PART TWO

LIFE IN THE EIGHTEENTH CENTURY

CHAPTER 5

GOVERNMENT AND RELIGION

THROUGHOUT the 18th century the King continued
to be the chief figure in the government of the country,
but he was a monarch who held his power because
Parliament granted it. He chose his own ministers,
but he could no longer keep them without Parliament's
consent. A royal favourite like Bute was unable to
stay in office, whereas Pitt came to power in spite of
George II's dislike of him.

Because, on occasion, the King understood that he
must bow to the will of Parliament, it was no longer
necessary to impeach an unpopular minister or to
cut off his head. When a minister had lost the confidence of Parliament, he merely resigned from his
office and was replaced by another.

Whigs and Tories, less organised than the parties of   *Politics*
today, were the two political groups of the century,
each with its leader and outstanding members.
Though Walpole himself never used the title, the

71

leader of the party in power came to be known as the Prime Minister, and the old Privy Council was known as the Cabinet. The members of the Cabinet, drawn from both Houses, all belonged to the same party, and they met regularly to discuss the country's affairs and to decide upon the laws and the taxes that should be put forward for the approval of Parliament. In theory, the King presided over Cabinet meetings, but since George I's inability to understand English had caused him to stay away, the Cabinet had been left to carry on its discussions without the monarch.

The Cabinet

Thus, our modern system of government took shape, though it is doubtful if the mass of Englishmen realised what was happening. Few of them had so much as a vote at election times, and those who had were usually prepared to use it according to the wishes of some great landowner like Newcastle. Yet the cases of Wilkes, of Captain Jenkins' ear and of Walpole's Excise Bill showed that popular opinion could influence the government.

Englishmen were fond of boasting of their liberties, though few had any clear idea of what these were, apart from the claim to say and often to write what they pleased. Although in religion, in their work and at law, they had none of the rights which nowadays are taken for granted, they were still the most outspoken and truculent people in Europe. No government, certainly no monarch and royal army, would have dared to rule them as the French and German people were ruled.

Parliament still represented only a tiny part of the nation. The House of Lords, numbering some 220 peers, including 26 bishops, had far more influence than today because its members were the most powerful men in the country. The House of Commons was composed of country gentlemen, merchants, lawyers, Army and Navy officers, a few writers like

A NAVAL OFFICER

ALDERMEN
AND COUN-
CILLORS AT
A BANQUET

Addison and Steele, and a handful of adventurers like Wilkes, who bought his first seat for £7000.

In the Commons there were about 80 county Members who were usually nominated by the powerful county families. These Members were mostly squires, more interested in their dogs and horses, their crops and neighbours than in the tedious proceedings at Westminster where they attended as seldom as possible. Besides them and the 45 Scottish Members were several hundred from those boroughs and cities which had the right to return one or two Members to Parliament.* Many large towns, especially in the North, had no representative at all, whereas tiny places, once important but now ruinous or almost uninhabited, still returned a Member. Landowners were able to control these " rotten boroughs ", where a handful of electors solemnly voted as they were bidden.

There was no clear right to vote. In the country districts, the only voters were men who held freehold land worth forty shillings a year—and there were precious few of them. In the towns, there was no uniform system, for in some places the voters were the Mayor, Alderman and Councillors ; in others, they

The House of Commons

Voters

* See footnote, page 211.

73

Parliament did not represent the people

were the householders, the local freemen or those who paid poor-rate. Almost all were solid men in business, in the professions or in occupation of land, for Parliament represented property, not people. The voters were few in number ; only 22 boroughs had as many as 1000 electors each, and 204 Members were returned to Parliament by total of 85,000 votes, just about 400 per seat. With voters so few, it was easy for great landowners to control elections, especially as there was rarely more than one candidate to vote for.

Yet, oddly enough, the system worked. Parliament was filled with men seeking their own advancement, but most were also devoted to their country. The great landlords who spent so freely to secure their own " pocket " candidates, were usually patriots who believed they were doing right for England. The Duke of Newcastle spent a fortune on elections and retired disappointed and much poorer. Love of power and a sense that politics was the proper occupation for wealthy men drove the Pitts, the Newcastles and the Walpoles to devote their lives to Parliament. They served their own class, but they were not blind to the interests of the country as a whole and, far from wishing to oppress the lowest classes, they believed that they were working to make England great and prosperous.

It was an age of orators, when men like Carteret, Henry Fox, Pitt and Chesterfield swayed the packed benches with the brilliance of their speeches, so that Parliament could, and sometimes did, rise above intrigue and jobbery.

The politician's view

The fault of the 18th-century politician was that he took the world as he found it and made no effort to reform it or to make it less harsh for the unfortunates. Such an idea seldom, if ever, occurred to him. It was his own class that owned land, that bought and sold the nation's merchandise, that was born to rule. As

for the mass of the people, it was their duty to recognise their " betters ", and to be content with the position in which God had placed them.

Unlike today, Parliament interfered as little as possible in local affairs. The Lord-Lieutenant of the county was a local magnate whose chief responsibility was the Militia, but the real rulers of the countryside were the Justices of the Peace.

Unpaid, and drawn largely from the upper-middle class, the J.P. carried out a remarkable range of duties. He was responsible for law and order, for the bridges, roads and jails in the district. He fixed wages, licensed various trades, imposed rates for the relief of the poor, recruited troops, appointed the constables and dealt with criminal and civil cases in Court, where he had the assistance of a jury. For various minor offences, such as swearing, poaching, drunkenness and vagrancy, he could fine a man or put him in the stocks without trial. There was no appeal against his judgement, except that the King's Judges might occasionally correct a major error, or in special circumstances, as in armed rebellion, the Secretary of State might assert the authority of the Crown.

The Justice of the Peace

Fortunately, most of the Justices of the Peace were honest men who were respected for their common sense and fatherly interest in their own districts. Undoubtedly some were overbearing tyrants, but in most cases the Squire was a kindly despot, like Sir Roger de Coverley, or a shrewd practical farmer, reasonably educated, surprisingly well-travelled, and devoted to his own patch of England.

In country districts the Squire's right-hand man was the Parson. There was a huge gulf between the Bishops with their large incomes (Durham had £6000 a year and Winchester £5000) and the lowly curates. Like the politicians, the higher clergy of the 18th

century were self-satisfied. There was, as yet, little zeal to comfort the wretched, or to carry the Gospel into the slums of the big cities and the growing towns of the North.

It was common for clergymen to hold more than one " living " (appointment) ; pocketing the greater part of the income, they employed ill-paid curates to carry out their duties. The son of Bishop Hoadly, for instance, obtained no fewer than five livings and four church appointments. Many livings belonged to the colleges of Oxford and Cambridge, many to county families and others to lay persons and companies, so that influence and favour were more important to a clergyman than godliness and the ability to preach.

The Parson

Enthusiasm for religion was out of fashion. The Parson christened, married and buried his parishioners ; he took services on Sundays, but not always twice on the same day. In the diocese of York in 1743 it was found that many churches had a service only fortnightly or monthly, with Holy Communion four times a year. Hymns were rare and church music was of a low standard ; sermons, in language far above the heads of the common people, were tediously long, and it was common for the clergyman to make or buy a collection of sermons to last him throughout his career.

If the Parson spent little time on his church duties, he was busy enough in everyday affairs. He farmed his glebe land, bought and sold cattle, entertained his neighbours and hunted with the local farmers and the Squire. He presided over the vestry meetings which elected the churchwardens, agreed the rates and ran the parish. Generally speaking he was regarded by his parishioners as one of their " betters ", a member of the gentry, to whom they paid their tithes and touched their hats.

HOGARTH'S VERSION
OF A
LONG SERMON

DISSENTERS WERE
ALLOWED TO RUN
SCHOOLS

Though a curate might receive as little as £20 a year, and Oliver Goldsmith wrote of a village parson that he " was passing rich on forty pounds a year ", clergymen were comfortably off compared with most of their flock. At a time when a labourer earned a shilling a day and a servant had five pounds a year and her keep, there were plenty of parsons with livings worth two or three hundred pounds, along with certain fees, a well-built vicarage, standing in several acres, with its barn, stables, dairy and fishpond.

In the eyes of the law, Roman Catholics were still outcasts. A priest who said Mass was guilty of treason, and a Catholic schoolmaster could be fined forty shillings a day for instructing the young. No Catholic could hold office in the State, could travel more than five miles, own a gun, attend a university, act as a doctor, lawyer, army or naval officer. In practice, the people and the J.P.s were less harsh than their laws, and Catholics were usually allowed to live in peace, though dread of their religion was still close to the surface, as the Gordon Riots proved in 1780.* *Catholics and Dissenters*

Dissenters, or Nonconformists, were treated more mildly. They were permitted to build their own meeting-houses which, Defoe noted on his travels,

* See footnote, page 117.

were crowded with earnest worshippers. Although the law did not allow Dissenters to sit in Parliament or on the local councils or to serve as officers in the armed forces, the Whigs saw to it that there was sufficient toleration for them to run their schools and businesses without difficulty.

Early in the 18th century it seemed as if the Dissenters might fade from the scene. The easy-going policy of the Whigs and the temptation for well-to-do Dissenters to go over to the Church of England had damped down the passionate zeal for religion that was so typical of the previous century. Yet, it was a movement which began inside the Church of England that brought new life to the Dissenting religion.

The Methodists

John Wesley (1703–1791) and his brother Charles, serious-minded young men at Oxford, formed a club at the university whose members were contemptuously nicknamed the " Methodists ". John Wesley believed that the simple truth of Christianity needed to be carried to people who had forgotten or had never known the message of the Gospels. Though he was, and always remained, a member of the Church of England, he was not concerned with matters of ceremony and ritual, or with the difference between High and Low churchmen. His single passionate aim was to bring the teachings of Christ into the lives of men and women, and he speedily found that the greatest need was among those for whom fox-hunting parsons and worldly bishops had little time. In the new towns of the North, in the slums, and in districts where there were mines and factories, people lived in squalid misery increased by the habit of drinking cheap gin.

At first, the Wesleys preached in churches, but as their enthusiasm roused the hostility of the clergy, they took to the open air, like their friend George Whitefield, a preacher of spell-binding power. With

WESLEY'S BIRTHPLACE AT EPWORTH, LINCOLNSHIRE

HOGARTH'S
CARICATURE OF
THE EFFECTS
OF GIN

a handful of friends to support him, John Wesley preached in market-places, at cross-roads, in fields and on the commons. He covered 250,000 miles in 50 years. He walked and rode up and down England, in rain and snow, through storms, floods and riots. He faced angry mobs and indignant Justices, he put up with hunger and discomfort, writing his books and pamphlets in the saddle, sending innumerable letters, encouraging his friends, training new preachers and organising the work to which he had given his life. Nothing could stop him ; not the jeers of workmen nor the disapproval of the Church. He preached to miners in Newcastle, in Cornwall and in Wales, to weavers in Yorkshire and East Anglia, to factory workers in the North, to labourers by the wayside, to soldiers on the march and to genteel folk at fashionable spas.

Charles Wesley, John's younger brother, became the greatest of all hymn-writers, composing 6500 hymns, of which some 500 are still sung today. Hymns like

Wesley preaches throughout England

JOHN WESLEY

" Hark the Herald Angels Sing ", " Jesu, lover of my Soul ", with Isaac Watts's " O God our Help in Ages Past ", had a tremendous effect on illiterate workers to whom the simple words came like messages from God.

Though he never wished it, the movement that Wesley inspired became separate from the Church of England. George Whitefield, the preacher, so influenced Selina, Countess of Huntingdon, that she spent a fortune on building chapels and training ministers in her Nonconformist beliefs.

Wesley's work triumphed. Methodism brought self-respect, patience and decency to thousands of workers at a time when many were in danger of sinking into despair or turning to revolutionary violence. By the end of the century, as Wesley hoped, a new zeal arose in the Church of England, when the " Evangelical Churchmen ", as they were called, took a deep interest in the poor, the maimed, the prisoners and the children.

From John Wesley can be traced the work of John Howard and Elizabeth Fry in the jails, of Wilberforce (1759–1833) for slaves, of Lord Shaftesbury for poor children, of the Church Missionary Society (1799), the British and Foreign Bible Society, and of the founders of church schools in the early years of the 19th century.

These efforts, and many more, to help less fortunate human beings are called " humanitarianism ". It was a movement that redeemed the selfishness of a harsh age, and its influence is still alive and strong today.

WESLEY
PREACHING

CHAPTER 6

AN EIGHTEENTH-CENTURY PARSON
IN HIS VILLAGE

THE Reverend James Woodforde was born in 1740
in Somerset, where his father was Rector of one parish
and Vicar of another. The Woodfordes were comfortably off, so young James went to school at Winchester,
and on to New College, Oxford, where he started the
Diary that, in sixty-eight neat little books, he was to
keep until his death in 1803.

At Oxford the pleasant young man took life easily,
and in due course became a clergyman like his father,
after an examination that lasted " quite half an hour ",
when the Bishop asked " a good many hard and deep
questions ".

From Oxford James returned to Somerset to become curate of a parish worth £40 a year. This was
only a temporary appointment, but he soon secured
another at £20, though Farmer Bower, the chief *A curate's salary*
parishioner, was annoyed to find that for this sum there
was to be only one service on Sundays, and he increased
the salary to £30 when Woodforde promised to
provide two services.

THE WOODFORDES'
PARSONAGE

Next year the diarist became curate to his own
father and moved into the " Lower House ", near the
family parsonage, with his brother Jack whose wild
drinking bouts and scandalous behaviour were a sore
trial to the gentle clergyman.

After his father died, James discovered that the
living had been given to a cousin. Rather disgruntled,
he went back to his old college at Oxford as Sub-
Warden and Pro-Proctor, which meant that he sometimes had to discipline students who had misbehaved
in the city. Not happy in this life, he applied for the
Mastership of Bedford School. This was a splendid
post, with a salary of 200 guineas, a new house, fuel,
candles, " all kind of expenses and no taxes whatso-
ever ", for teaching 12 boys with the help of an Usher.
Unfortunately, the college awarded this plum to
another.

However, all turned out well. A rector died in
Norfolk, leaving vacant a good living " in the gift " of
New College. Woodforde and a Mr. Hooke applied
for it and, after the Senior Members had debated the
matter for 2 hours, it was put to a vote and Woodforde,
sensibly voting for himself, was successful.

Thus, 34 years old, James became rector of Weston
Longeville, a parish some ten miles from Norwich, and
there, with his niece as housekeeper, the kindly

82

bachelor was to stay for 27 years. It was an unremarkable life in a quiet backwater, and we should know nothing of Parson Woodforde if he had not set down in his Diary, almost as though he were talking to himself, the everyday happenings of a country parish in 18th-century England.

SERVANTS AND WAGES

The parsonage, a thatched house with its parlour, dining-room, study and kitchen, was probably the largest building in the parish apart from the church and Weston House, where Squire Custance lived with his pretty wife, his numerous children and a dozen or more servants and grooms.

The Parson's household

The parson, too, lived in some style, for his household consisted of himself, his plump niece, Nancy, and five servants. There was the upper-maidservant who did the cooking, a maid-of-all-work whose duties included the daily milking, a man-servant to wait at table and look after his master, and the farm-servant, faithful Ben Leggatt, who worked the parson's glebe land. These four lived in at the rectory, together with a boy of about eleven or twelve who ran errands, fetched, carried and generally made himself useful, and thus earned his title "Skipjack".

SERVANTS WERE HIRED
AT MICHAELMAS

Servants

Servants were hired at Michaelmas for a year at a time, and were paid yearly in January, though they expected and received tips on various occasions and from visitors. In addition, they were fed, housed, and well supplied with beer, but wines and spirits were not provided for servants.

Tea, at 10s. 6d. a pound from Smuggler Andrews, was a luxury that might be specially agreed upon for an upper servant, while, from a generous master, there were occasional gifts of dress-lengths for the maids, waistcoat-cloth for the men and, for " Briton " Scurl, the manservant, a brown suit with a top coat to match. However, a servant's hours were long, and there were holidays only when the master gave permission for a day off to visit the gingerbread fair, or to attend a harvest " frolic " or a hanging at the crossroads. Ben Leggatt was often in Norwich at the market, and Briton was constantly to and fro, delivering messages, collecting the letters and buying goods for the household.

Parson Woodforde paid the following wages to his " folk " :

A maid	£ 3 3s. 0d. a year
An 18-year-old maid in her first post	£ 2 10s. 0d. a year
An upper-maidservant	£ 5 5s. 0d. and tea twice daily
Ben Leggatt, the farm servant	£10 a year (for which Ben not only farmed the parson's fields, but sold his corn, hay, turnips and pigs at Norwich and came trustily home with the money)

A MAIDSERVANT WITH
A WARMING-PAN

A manservant	£ 5 5s. od. a year, increased to £8 for Briton Scurl, who stayed 18 years
A Boy (Skipjack)	£ 1 1s. od. a year, later £2 2s. od. (The boys only stayed a year or two and left at about 14 to " better themselves ")
A labourer	£ 0 1s. 6d. a day
Washerwoman	£ 0 0s. 6d. a day and food.
A rat-catcher	£ 0 10s. 6d. for his work
To the Schoolmaster for teaching 2 servants to read and write	£ 0 4s. 6d. a quarter each

Besides wages, the parson had to pay a tax on his servants, £2 10s. for a male and 10 shillings for a female. This was one of the many devices to raise money for England's increasing expenditure during the wars with the American colonies and France. Besides the old land-tax and poor rate, there were taxes on riding-horses, dogs, hair-powder for wigs, and windows. We find that the parson, who was also taxed for being a bachelor, employed a couple of men to brick up three windows in order to reduce his taxes, and he had a mild grumble about the double duty on wines. When Mr. Pitt brought in his dreadful Income Tax, Parson Woodforde felt that it was enough to charge himself £20, whereas the rightful sum should have been more like £30, i.e., 10 per cent of his income.

THE PARSON HAD THREE
WINDOWS BRICKED UP

The Tithe Frolic

Weston was a very comfortable living, for every December the seventeen or so local farmers brought along to the parsonage their tithes amounting to about £285. Each year the occasion was celebrated by the Tithe Frolic, when a huge sirloin of roast beef, a leg of boiled mutton and " plumb puddings " were served, together with wine, punch, ale and rum, and followed by many " droll songs " and alas, at times, some misbehaviour and quarrelling.

EATING AND DRINKING

The parsonage was a bustling, cheerful household, busier with farming, with preparing food, drink and the entertainment of visitors than with church affairs. Parson Woodforde took service twice on Sundays, but after an illness in his fifties, he employed a curate at £30 a year to carry out most of his duties, and he generally found himself too poorly to attend church on Sunday, though he was often surprisingly well on Monday. For his day, however, he was a good parson and a kindly one, doing his duty to God in much the same way as to King George, whose birthday he honoured by firing an old blunderbuss into the air.

The parson's recreation

The parson's heart was really in his neat little estate. Most days he was out in his garden, extending the " pleasure grounds ", planting a tree, seeing to the cleaning out of the pond and the pruning of fruit trees. He walked into his fields to watch Ben ploughing or to encourage the villagers harvesting his wheat and barley. There was beer to be brewed, a pig to be killed, one of the cows was about to calve, and he must bleed the horses because neither was well, and he had some skill as an animal doctor. The parson enjoyed coursing with his greyhounds, Minx, Hector, Snip and Rover, but if hares were out of season, there were fish in his own pond and in the river Wensum at the end of the garden.

DINNER AT THE
PARSONAGE

Thus, the parsonage produced a good deal of its own food and the rest came in from Norwich, for the village had no shop of its own. Inside the house, the servants spent most of their time preparing and cooking mountains of food. The gentry ate meat—fish, poultry, game, mutton and beef. Boiled, roasted or baked meat came first. Bread came a poor second, but vegetables were less despised than formerly now that salads were fashionable, though potatoes were usually ignored by " the quality ". An assortment of cakes, tarts, jellies and custards usually came on at the end of dinner for those who fancied them.

The parson loved his stomach and rarely failed to note down what he had eaten, " Dinner today, boiled Beef & a rost Chicken ", but a dinner-party called for greater detail. One day, *six* people sat down at his table and he gave them :

" for dinner a dish of fine Tench, Ham and 3 Fowls boiled, a Plumb Pudding, a couple of Ducks roasted, a roasted neck of Pork, a Plumb Tart and an Apple Tart. Pears, Apples and Nutts after dinner. White Wine and Red, Beer and Cyder. Coffee and Tea in the evening at six, Hashed Fowl and Duck and Eggs and Potatoes etc. for supper. We did not dine till four o'clock, nor supped till ten."

A meal for six persons

Naturally enough, any unusual dish was noted in the Diary. The parson ate " a Pine Apple " for the first time ; his household vastly enjoyed a great pike " roasted with a pudding in his belly " ; the Squire sent a fine cucumber and a hen-pheasant ; the first green Peas of the season were served—" Thank God ! I was finely today," murmured the Parson. Once he went to dinner with the Squire and tasted a new dish :

> " a fine Swan rosted with Currant Jelly Sauce for the first Course.
> The second Course a couple of Wild Fowl called Dun Fowls, Larks, Blamange, Tarts etc. etc. and a good Desert of Fruit amongst which was a Damson Cheese. I never eat a bit of Swan before, and I think it good eating with sweet sauce."

But if the gentry ate well, they drank even more. Beer and cider were brewed at home, but the parson was forever buying wines, and there were regular deliveries of rum and gin from the smugglers. Sometimes at night there was a low whistle outside, followed by a thud on the ground and a discreet tap at the window. When the back door was opened there was no one to be seen, but a tub of rum stood on the doorstep. The Diary noted, " had 2 Tubb of Geneva [gin] brought me this evening by Moonshine, 4 gallons each Tub ". Soon afterwards there was great agitation and " bad reports about the Parish " because someone had informed on Buck the blacksmith, agent of the smugglers. The parson, having had a tub delivered the previous night, " got up very early this Morning and was very busy all this Morn in very necessary business ", which doubtless consisted of bottling the " moonshine " and hiding it away.

WINE GLASSES

Smugglers and the Parson

Buck, the blacksmith, was let off lightly by the Court, because gentry and commoners alike, including clergymen, considered that there was no harm in smuggling, and it was only rated a crime by unreasonable people like Mr. Pitt.

All classes drank heavily, and although there had *Drink* been some control over the ruinous drinking of cheap spirits, gin still cost the parson only £1 3s. for *nineteen* bottles. Port wine was not much dearer, being 1s. 6d. a quart bottle in 1774, though with Mr. Pitt's double duties, the price had risen to 2s. 9d. in 1798, " an amazing Price indeed ". The parson, like the Prime Minister and many of the gentry, suffered from gout through excessive drinking of port, and although he sometimes vowed to drink no more than three or four glasses a day, any kind of sickness or cold called forth the bottle.

Drunkenness was very common. It caused innumerable accidents, quarrels and crimes. John Woodforde, the wild young brother, was constantly in trouble, singing, swearing and making " an intolerable noise " half the night. Several times he had bad falls from his horse when coming home, and once this also happened to old Ben Leggatt, who wandered about all night looking for his horse. It was a recognised thing for Ben to come home drunk after he had been round the parish to inform the farmers of the date of the Tithe Frolic. Will Colman, manservant, had to be dismissed for his drunken ways, and even Briton, who stayed 18 years nearly lost his job several times when he became saucy through drink.

THE OLD BELL INN,
HOLBORN

The Englishman had long been renowned for his hard drinking, but there were few periods in history when drunkenness was more widespread than in the 18th century. It was easy to say that drink dulled the misery of the poor, but " drunk as a lord " was looked upon as a common and an enviable state. The gentry at dinner and in their London clubs, coachmen on their boxes, soldiers and sailors on and off duty, the mob pouring out of their hovels with clubs and brickbats, were all stupid or violent from drink. The reason was that liquor was both cheap and strong, for tea-drinking as yet had little appeal and the taverns were open from dawn until far into the night.

SOCIAL CLASSES

In his snug little world the Parson was a kindly, gentle tyrant. He was hurt when his niece or the servants were pert, but from time to time he screwed up his courage and spoke severely to Nancy or Briton. He dismissed a lazy boy, a maid who could not cook, a tipsy manservant and " a saucy swearing lad " who would not work unless he was watched.

But for the most part he was an affectionate master, who grieved when poor Molly Dade, best of all maids, died of consumption. He was sorry when Tim went off to join the army and he gave Billy Downing, " a very good lad ", five shillings when he walked to Norwich and back to buy a pair of breeches. There were gifts and extras for all his " folk ", and most of them served him for years.

Kind and generous as he was, the Parson knew exactly where everyone stood in society. Class barriers were higher than in Stuart times, and wealth separated the " betters " from the wage-earners and the destitute. Servants had to " know their place ", and the humbler kind of farming man took supper in the kitchen,

EIGHTEENTH-CENTURY ARMCHAIRS

WESTON HOUSE, THE
HOME OF SQUIRE CUSTANCE

alongside John Smith, the parish clerk. Tradesmen and shopkeepers stood higher than servants, but lower than prosperous farmers. The Parson, usually considered one of the gentry (unless he was poor and therefore despised), had deep respect for the Squire, and it was the Squire, in his solid Georgian mansion, who ruled the countryside.

Up at Weston House, Squire Custance and his wife were all that country gentry should be. Connected with the nobility, having business at Court and a house in Bath, they still loved their Norfolk estate and were devoted to its gardens and fields, to sport, to the church and the village. They were generous to the poor, kind to Nancy and genteel to her uncle.

When there were noble visitors at the big house, or a christening party in honour of a newly arrived baby, the Parson and Nancy were sure to be invited. Immediately after the child had been " named " (this ceremony was carried out at home and was distinct from a christening in church), Squire Custance would quietly slip into the Parson's hand a five-guinea Norwich Bank Note, " wrapped in a clean piece of writing paper ". Some of the babies died, but seven children *The Squire and* lived to grow up ; gentle Mrs. Custance fell ill and *his family* all the family moved to Bath for her health. At last, she was better, and when they came back to Norfolk to open up the big house, the whole village and its now ailing parson rejoiced to have them home.

91

THE POOR

The poor of the parish were very numerous, when one considers that England was the richest country in Europe. The population of the village was about 360, and when on St. Thomas's Day in December, the parson gave sixpence to each " poor person ", the number was usually between 50 and 60. Since these must have been adults, and it is unlikely that he gave to more than one member of a family, it is easy to see that at least half the parish could be considered " poor ".

It went without saying that a labourer, even in regular work, could barely support himself and his family above starvation level. Given reasonable weather and health, he earned about £18 a year, but since his rent, fuel and tools cost about £3 and his own food £9 (the figure which farmers reckoned as the cost of a servant's keep), there was only £6 a year left to feed and clothe his wife and children. No wonder so many children died in infancy ; no wonder wives worked in the fields and trudged 12 miles to earn a few coppers as washerwomen. Children helped with the harvest for the free food and went crow-scaring as soon as they could walk. Illness, old age, bad weather or the loss of the family cow were disasters that could be relieved only by charity.

Low wages were eked out by Poor Relief, so that Parson Woodforde's poor rate increased from £1 5s. 2½d. for the half-year in 1784 to £2 5s. 4½d. in 1796, and £6 13s. in 1800. These large increases were caused partly by bad harvests and hard winters, and also after 1795, by the odious *Speenhamland* practice. The magistrates of that village in Berkshire decided to give parish relief according to the price of bread. The plan was widely

WAGES IN THE COUNTRY WERE SO LOW THAT MANY PEOPLE WERE FORCED TO GO TO THE TOWNS TO LOOK FOR WORK

adopted, with disastrous results. Farmers continued
to pay low wages, and the proud industrious labourer
found himself worse off than the man who accepted
a pauper's dole. The rates rose so high that small
farmers could not afford to pay and land went out of
cultivation. By 1817 poor relief amounted to the
staggering figure of nearly £8 million for a population
of 11 million.

Our parson did what he could for the poor, without
unduly hurting himself. On St. Valentine's Day all
the children who came to the rectory, 50 or 60 of
them, had a penny each for saying " Good Morrow,
Valentine "; on Christmas Day he gave dinner and a
shilling each to several old people, and he often sent a
plate of meat to a sick parishioner, a basket of fruit to
another and clothes to several more. During a winter
so terrible that milk froze indoors and two women
died when walking home from market, the Parson sent
for the Overseer of the Poor and gave him £10 to spend
as he thought best. Altogether £46 15s. was raised
in the parish to buy bread and coal, which were doled
out at the church door after service on Sundays.
Besides the poor in the parish, there were beggars on
the road who called at the Parsonage, and seldom
went away empty-handed. The Diary is full of such
notes as, " To a poor travelling woman, gave 1.0 ",
" To a poor man out of work and a very cleanly old
Man, gave 0.6 ", and " To a poor Sailor, having lost
his left hand, gave 1.0 ".

The destitute poor were sometimes sent to the
Workhouse, a place utterly dreaded by all self-respecting folk. Parson Woodforde called at the House of
Industry at Dereham, " a very large building . . . about
380 Poor in it now, but they don't look either healthy
or cheerful, a great Number die there, 27 have died
since Christmas last ", and once he gave a shilling to
" a very civil spoken Man " who had escaped from

A NIGHT
WATCHMAN

The workhouse

Bargewell Poor House, " being hardly kept alive there, the Allowance so very short, the House being farmed out at 1s. 6d. per week for each poor Person ".

Despite poverty, crime seems to have been almost non-existent in country districts compared with London. In more than forty years the Diary hardly mentions a crime worthy of the name. A man called Biggin stole some wood, and seven years later the same fellow, " an old offender ", was whipped through the street for stealing potatoes. In Norfolk, some highwaymen were captured and there were rumours of rogues stealing chickens and the like ; the parson's stable was broken into and a hatchet, a bridle, a hook and a pair of Ben's hedging gloves were taken. But in a district where everyone knew everyone else, the robbers were soon caught. Wars, poverty, beggars on the roads, riots in London and revolutionary talk everywhere, but at the parsonage there was only that one petty robbery in 27 years. Servants came and went ; some were dismissed for their drinking or their saucy ways, boys were sent packing for swearing and idling, but not one for dishonesty.

TRAVELLING

Travel by coach Every three or four years Parson Woodforde took a long holiday to visit his relatives and friends in Somer-

set. Having arranged for a neighbouring clergyman to carry out his duties, he hired a post chaise to Norwich, with his niece and manservant, and there took the night coach to London.

This coach left the Angel Inn at 9.0 p.m. and made the 109-mile journey through the darkness in 17 hours, reaching " The Swan and Two Necks " in London at two o'clock in the afternoon. The coach carried six passengers inside and as many as could cling to the outside, together with a great deal of luggage, and it must have travelled at a spanking rate. The Norwich-London road was one of the best in the kingdom, and the fact that regular night-runs could be made shows that the roads were now reasonably free from high-waymen.

In London the travellers usually stayed at an inn called the " Bell Savage ", which bore out Arthur Young's view that most inns were " dirty and dear ". The parson, however, did not complain ; even when he was so bitten by bed-bugs that his face and hands swelled up. Four years later, he stayed at the same inn, kept by the same " very civil people ", and this time the bugs forced him to get up at 4.0 a.m. and go for a walk, and for the next two nights he did not undress but dozed in a chair with his feet up.

A dirty inn

After seeing the sights of the capital, and once being frightened by the mob who insulted King George III and broke the windows of his coach, the Woodfordes went on to Bath. They travelled by an exceptionally speedy vehicle, " called the Balloon Coach on Account of its travelling so fast, making it a point to be before the Mail Coach ". This coach carried four passengers inside and was pulled by only a pair of horses. In

THE NIGHT
COACH FROM
NORWICH

1786 it left London at 7.0 in the evening, but in 1793, when Briton travelled on the roof, the journey was by day, starting at 5 o'clock in the morning.

Travelling companions

" We had a very fat Woman with a Dog and many band boxes, which much incommoded us, and also a poor sickly good kind of Man that went with us. We breakfasted at Maidenhead on Coffee & Tea. For Strawberries at Maidenhead, paid 1.0. For our breakfast, paid 2.0. We were very near meeting with an Accident in Reading, passing a Waggon, but thank God we got by safe and well. It was owing to the Coachman . . . At Reading there were two young Gentlemen by name Joliffe that got on top of the Coach, being going home from School for the Vacation. I remembered their father at Winchester School. We dined at the Pelican Inn Speenham Land. . . . About 10 o'clock this evening, thank God, we got safe and well to Bath to the White Hart Inn, where we supped & slept—a very noble Inn."

Sometimes the Woodfordes lingered for a day or two in fashionable Bath, calling on friends, including Squire Custance and family, visiting the famous Pump Room, the Play House and Simpson's Room where they attended a Ball, " very elegant indeed ". The last part of the journey into Somerset, being off

THE COACH
ALWAYS
STOPPED AT
AN INN

a main route, had to be completed by post-chaise, hired from the inn. There was seldom any difficulty about this, for every inn of any size stabled fifty or more horses and usually had several chaises available. On one occasion, however, the Woodfordes found themselves held up for lack of fresh horses and were kept waiting in company with Mr. Pitt himself, Prime Minister of England.

The cost of travel was very high indeed. Here, made up from the pages of the Diary, is the bill for the journey from Norfolk to Somerset in 1786, when the Parson was accompanied by Nancy and Nephew Bill :

THE CHURCH OF
ST. MARY-LE-BOW
IN LONDON

		£	s.	d.
Weston to Norwich	Postchaise and dinner	1	0	6*
Norwich to London	3 " inside " places @ 30s.	4	10	0
	Extra luggage		15	0
	Breakfasts en route		3	0
	Tips to coachmen		6	0
In London	Bell Savage Inn (4 days)	3	10	6
	Tips to servants at inn		10	6
London to Bath	3 " inside " places	4	10	0
	Breakfasts		4	0
	Extra luggage		13	0
	Coachman and guard		5	0
Bath to Shepton Mallet (Somerset)	Castle Inn (1 night), breakfast, post-chaise	2	7	4½
	Driver		3	0
Shepton Mallet to Cole.	Post-chaise and turnpike		12	6
	Total	£19	10	4½

Cost of a journey

* This item was not mentioned in 1786, but in other years the charge was about £1.

ENG. BK. III—7

The return journey to Norfolk, via Salisbury and London was not quite so expensive, because Nephew Bill did not travel back with the Parson and his niece, but the total for the round trip came to about £35— as much as a farm worker would earn in two years or a maidservant in six or seven.

When, in his younger days, the Parson rode on horseback from Norfolk to Somerset, the six-day journey was of course much cheaper, the cost for himself, his man and two horses coming to £6 3s. 3½d. By far the most expensive form of travel was post-chaise, which seems to have cost anything from one to two shillings a mile, but there was no other means, except the carrier's cart, for travellers with luggage who lived off the regular coach routes.

AMUSEMENTS

Although Nancy sometimes complained to her uncle that life was dull in a country parsonage, there was a variety of entertainment for those with well-lined pockets and a stout little horse to take them to Norwich.

An early balloonist   There were elections, frolics and musical evenings in the city. There was the occasion, in 1785, when " amid a vast Concourse of People ", they saw Mr. Decker and his Balloon sail majestically into the air, and disappear beyond the trees. There was sometimes a Grand Procession through the streets in honour of Peace and of Bishop Blaise, patron saint of

WHEN THE PARSON WAS
YOUNGER HE TRAVELLED
ON HORSEBACK

the wool trade, with Hercules, the Golden Fleece, the Militia Band, horses, chariots, drummers and trumpeters.

Norwich possessed a theatre, where Mrs. Siddons, the famous actress, appeared occasionally, and here, in 1794, after a play called *School for Wives* and the usual " entertainment " (a knock-about comedy to enliven the proceedings), the parson heard " the song of God Save the King sung with great Glee ". Every now

THE PARSON SOMETIMES WENT TO THE THEATRE IN NORWICH

and again there was a Music Festival supported by subscriptions from gentry to attract London performers. At one such Grand Concert, Madame Mara sang delightfully and there were " near 100 performers " in the Orchestra. Next morning, in St. Peter's Church, Madame Mara and her company sang in superb style an oratorio by Handel. The church was packed, and Norwich so full that it was said two rooms were let for 10 guineas.

The theatre was considered to be more respectable than in Stuart times, and only the stricter Dissenters looked upon play-going as a sinful occupation. Out-of-the-way places which nowadays seldom, if ever, see the production of a play, had visits from travelling companies. Down in Somerset, for example, near the Woodforde home, " *Hamlet* ", " *As You Like It* ", " *Richard III* " and "*The Beggar's Opera* " were put on in the village Court House. Probably the acting was poor and the shabby players were glad enough to

Play-going

99

carn a supper, but it was real theatre and the local people came to see Shakespeare, and to guffaw at such supporting " entertainment " as " *Hob-in-the-Well* ", with its time-old clowning and horseplay.

In London, of course, plays were more polished, but there were not many theatres and no long runs. Most plays ran for only two or three nights ; five nights meant that a play paid its way, and ten success-ive nights meant a real success. As a result, there were plenty of plays ; a few, by Goldsmith and Sheridan, were witty and clever, some were bad, and the old favourites, especially versions of Shakespeare, were played over and over again. At the theatres money was not paid at the door, but at the end of the first act, when some of the hard-up could leave without paying. Another custom was for footmen to be admitted free to the top gallery, where they often disturbed the play with rowdy behaviour, but since they were needed to attend their masters and mistresses after the perform-ance, it was difficult to call them to order.

Curious entertainments

Once, in 1786, the parson took his niece to the circus in London, a new form of entertainment which con-sisted largely of skilful horsemanship, but in Norwich there were humbler entertainments, like the dwarf, the woman with no arms, and the Learned Pig that spelt out words from letters placed in front of it. Occasion-ally there was a more intellectual exercise than even the Learned Pig could provide ; at the Assembly Rooms, for instance, the parson heard a Lecture on Astronomy, " spoken by one Walker, with a View of his Eiduranion of transparent Orrery "—whatever that meant. People loved to see anything rare or curious, so there was a living to be made by wandering showmen who called at the parsonage and, for a shilling, allowed the household to peep into a box containing a child with two heads or to see " a pretty kind of monkey ", a mongoose from Madagascar.

At home, the Parson loved a game of cards, such as cribbage, whist, quadrille (a fore-runner of whist) and a game called Commerce. His winnings and losses were carefully entered in the Diary : " at Quadrille this Evening, lost 0.0.6 ", or " At Cribbage with Nancy, won 0.2.0. She was very sulky and sullen on losing it, tho' not paid."

Gadding about in London or Norwich, visiting the theatre, dining with the Bishop or Squire Custance were all very fine, but, confessed the parson, " being with our equals is much more agreeable ". Nothing could compare with a dinner-party at home, when the table groaned with food, the bottles went round, Briton waited at table and Betty and Molly were a-flutter with excitement in the kitchen. There were prim evenings with fellow clergymen, and boisterous ones too, like the wet evening when the parson and some of his guests sat up playing cards all night, while the rest shared the bedrooms, until roused at six o'clock in the morning by a serenade from the card-players. Once, on New Year's Eve, the company " were very merry indeed after Supper ", and Nancy and her friends locked the parson in the great Parlour and then fell on him and pulled his wig to pieces in the scrimmage. On another occasion they made him an " Apple Pye " bed, and stayed up singing all night long.

Merriment at the Parsonage

A RIOTOUS EVENING AT
THE PARSONAGE

EVERYDAY AFFAIRS

These jovial evenings were part of the round of life that went on, year in and year out, in country parishes all over England. Winters are still cold in Norfolk, but in Parson Woodforde's time they seem to have been particularly severe, and the parsonage was so cold that water froze indoors. Most people, even the poor, had to rely on coal for their heating, but coal was dear and had to be brought in heavy wagons from Norwich.

Summers seem to have been uncommonly hot, and there was always a good deal of illness, much of it caused no doubt by tainted food and impure water. Remedies were strange : " Nancy continues still to get better by drinking plentifully of Port Wine, at least 1 Pint in a day ", and " My Boy Jack had another touch of the Ague . . . I gave him a dram of Gin at the beginning of the fit and pushed him headlong into one of my ponds, and ordered him to bed immediately."

Ague, gout, stomach upsets, measles, consumption and even Malaria (called " the Whirligigousticon ") were common enough, but small-pox was dreaded most of all. For this, Doctor Thorne was inoculating villagers in the arm as early as 1776, twenty-two years before Jenner published his paper on vaccination, but Dr. Thorne's treatment contrasts with such quaint notions as the parson's remedy for a sty on his eyelid :

" as it is commonly said that the Eyelid being rubbed by the tail of a black Cat would do it much good, and having a black Cat, a little before Dinner, I made a trial of it and very soon after dinner I found my Eyelid much abated of the swelling and almost free from Pain ".

Sounds from the world beyond Weston occasionally ruffled its peaceful surface. Briton was sent into Norwich for letters and news : there were terrible

GEORGIAN SILVER

riots in London, there was fighting against the colonists in America and a revolution in France where, horror of horrors, the King was beheaded. The war was always going badly, except on the sea ; Tim ran away to join the Army, the Press Gang carried off a man from the very next village, there were rumours of a great riot planned to take place in Norwich and the French might invade any day. But the gentry stood firm and sensible. The militia was strengthened and even Briton and Ben Leggatt were enrolled in the cause of law and order. The news of Nelson's victories put new heart in everybody, especially in Norfolk, where his father was a parson. Nelson's cousins, the Sucklings, called one day upon Parson Woodforde and took dinner at his house.

But as always, the life of the village went on. The harvest had to be got in while fine weather lasted, Ben carted barley all day, the cow Beauty had a calf, and Briton helped his master to brew a barrel of Table-beer. Mr. Dade read prayers and preached in the church on Sunday, the weather was uncommonly dry and the old parson writing in his Diary in the rectory, noted, " for Dinner, boiled Beef and a Partridge roasted, etc."

CHAPTER 7

EIGHTEENTH-CENTURY TASTE
AND BEHAVIOUR

THE ARTS

There were a good many sides of 18th-century life about which a country clergyman knew little or nothing. As a traveller, Parson Woodforde did not venture outside the triangle of Norwich-London-Somerset : he never went abroad, or experienced the delights and dangers of the Grand Tour.

The Grand Tour   It was usual for a young man of means to complete his education by travelling in Europe. The Grand Tour varied from a few weeks in France to a protracted journey through the Netherlands to Paris and on to Switzerland, Germany and Italy. Young men like Boswell and Horace Walpole spent a year or more travelling abroad with a tutor or a group of companions. They stayed at inns or took rooms, but were often the guests of the local nobility and of English exiles who, for one reason or another, were to be found in the principal cities of France and Italy.

Among the gentry of most countries, except perhaps Spain, there was little nationalism. The ruling class welcomed their equals from other countries, so that an English " milord ", accompanied by his valet, and with his letters of introduction, his golden guineas or banker's notes in his pocket, could readily enter the polite society of Padua, Frankfurt or Geneva. It was common for Englishmen to travel in France and to be entertained in Paris salons, even when France and England were officially at war. But if the sons of English squires and noblemen often made themselves ridiculous abroad by their arrogance and by their weakness for wine and ladies, many of them also brought back much to enrich their own country.

A TROMBONE,
A BASSOON AND
A POCKET VIOLIN

The fashionable passion for ancient remains, for pictures and other artistic treasures was even stronger than the modern tourist's love of souvenirs. Statues, busts, urns and pillars were hauled back from Italy to ornament many an English garden and drawing-room, and old Masters, genuine or faked, were hung alongside the family portraits. Ideas about buildings, music, poetry and philosophy also came into England, along with more civilised notions about behaviour in polite society.

Architects such as Vanbrugh and Robert Adam drew inspiration from classical ruins in Italy and from the remains of Roman Emperor Diocletian's vast palace. This was the period when great mansions were built in wide parklands, with stately pillared

Architects

A MID-EIGHTEENTH-
CENTURY TOWN HOUSE
IN SOHO SQUARE,
LONDON

fronts and symmetrical wings to house the servants and horses. The eighteenth century is equally renowned for the smaller town and country houses which, in their mellow dignity, seem to be exactly suited to the prosperous folk who lived in them. There is hardly a town which does not still possess at least some of these houses, with their white-painted sash windows, and their brickwork the colour of ripe peaches. They possess something of Dutch neatness and charm, for the influence of Holland was considerable in a period that included a Dutch king on our throne.

A PIANO AND
A " SERPENT "

Later in the century, styles became more ornate, and Horace Walpole's enthusiasm for the " Gothick " was to have an unhappy effect on domestic architecture.

The magnificence of Versailles aroused the admiration of many Englishmen, so that French taste influenced the decoration of rooms and the design of furniture. This could be seen in the work of Sheraton and, to a lesser degree, in the designs of Chippendale and Heppelwhite.

Gardens

Versailles also influenced the lay-out of the gardens of great houses. Terraces, fountains and lakes formed a setting for the mansion. The passion for avenues of trees was so great that one wealthy landowner actually applied to Parliament for permission to plant an avenue all the way from Northamptonshire to London.

GEORGIAN
" GOTHICK " :
THE TEMPLE
AT STOWE

William Kent brought the park right up to the house, and even the surrounding country was " landscaped " by men like " Capability " Brown, who placed temples, grottoes, tumbling streams and artificial ruins to look " natural ", though the cost was often ruinous.

WILLIAM KENT

In music, Handel and the Italian opera dominated 18th-century taste, so that English music, once the best in Europe, was almost extinguished, apart from such " low " exceptions as John Gay's *The Beggar's Opera* (1728) and the patriotic and sentimental songs loved by the common people.

At the beginning of the period, English art was at a low ebb, but before the 18th century was out, painting had become highly esteemed. The Royal Academy was founded, and at least three of our greatest artists had established themselves. William Hogarth had a genius for depicting the people of his time ; his pictures of low life have a startling brutality that has only been approached by Thomas Rowlandson (1756–1827). But their pot-bellied citizens and pitiful revellers were not fashionable subjects for paint. This was the golden age of the portrait-painter, when every man of standing and wealth wanted a likeness of himself and his family.

" CAPABILITY " BROWN

In the homes of wealthy patrons, the rooms were large and therefore the portraits had to be large too. Paintings, known as " conversation pieces ", seven or eight feet high, showed the sitter surrounded by his family and dogs, often with a favourite horse as well, and in the background stood his house and its parkland. These groups of carefully arranged figures seem to be chatting together with the easy confidence of the ruling class. Sir Joshua Reynolds (1723–92) was the greatest of the portrait-painters, and his rivals included Gainsborough, Romney, George Stubbs, who excelled with horses, and Zoffany, a German artist.

HANDEL

Landscape painting was not yet fashionable. Richard Wilson almost starved and Gainsborough's country scenes remained unsold. But, by the end of the century, Constable (1776–1837) was painting the first of his masterpieces, and Cotman, Cox and Turner, were beginning to change the style and subjects of painting.

Writers and poets   As with painters, writers for the most part relied upon the support of wealthy persons who frequently subscribed a sum apiece for the writing or translating of a particular book. It would be dedicated to the chief patron, with an introduction or poem in his honour. Thus, most writers and poets spoke to a select society of the fashionable world, and their work had elegance but little heart. Dryden (d. 1700) and Pope (1688–1744) brought polished verse to perfection, and though their successors Samuel Johnson and Goldsmith sometimes mocked polite society, it was mockery that was seldom savage. William Cowper (1731–1800), best known for *John Gilpin*, showed in his serious poems a greater understanding of the gulf between that elegant world and the misery of the poor which Wesley strove to comfort.

Among 18th-century poets, perhaps because of this inner struggle, there was a strain of melancholy, and even of madness, that we find in William Collins, in Cowper himself, in that strange genius William Blake and in Thomas Gray, whose *Elegy Written in a Country Churchyard* has been quoted more than any poem in the language. In Parson Woodforde's time, Robert Burns (1759–1796) was writing his angry verses and the immortal love songs, but by the end of the century a new kind of poetry, quite different from Pope's, arrived with Wordsworth's *Lyrical Ballads*, to which Coleridge contributed *The Rhyme of the Ancient Mariner*.

WILLIAM
WORDSWORTH

In prose, Addison and Steele wrote about the

manners of quaint and genial persons to please an audience of squires and merchants, while Gibbon, the historian, Lord Chesterfield and Horace Walpole, the famous letter-writers, wrote for the educated society to which they themselves belonged. Daniel Defoe, however, often remembered only for *Robinson Crusoe* (1719), did much to found the popular journalism which Londoners demanded. A Swiss traveller noticed that " all Englishmen are great newsmongers. Workmen habitually begin the day by going to coffee-rooms in order to read the daily news ". This was in 1727, when there were at least sixteen London newspapers, as well as various magazines, and, in the rest of Britain, twenty-five provincial newspapers.

ROBERT BURNS, THE SCOTTISH POET

Jonathan Swift, author of *Gulliver's Travels*, was another who did not write to entertain an upper-class public, for, in the bitter sadness of his mind, he saw the follies and dirt beneath the surface of elegant plenty.

From the essays, letters and travellers' tales emerged the novel. Samuel Richardson, author of *Pamela* (1740), is usually regarded as our first novelist, and he was followed by Henry Fielding (1701–1754) the Bow Street magistrate who wrote *Tom Jones*, by Smollett with his rogues and seamen, by Laurence Sterne a half crazy clergyman, and a school of " terror " writers whose work continues in present-day crime stories. Then, with Jane Austen, born in 1775, (though *Pride and Prejudice* did not appear until 1813), the novel reached an artistic level that has rarely been surpassed.

The novel

Over the literary scene of the 18th century broods the vast figure of Doctor Johnson (1709–84). Growling, rumbling, belching, he sits straddle-legged in his London coffee-house, his wig awry, his clothes crumpled and stained, his person none too clean, as he booms out to the assembled company his views on life and

SAMUEL TAYLOR COLERIDGE

JAMES BOSWELL
AND DOCTOR
JOHNSON

Science

Steam-power

manners. The best-known writers of the day gather about him in delight, and often in dismay, at his crushing wit and thunderous rebukes. Johnson, creator of the famous *Dictionary* and of poems and essays now largely forgotten, was made immortal by the biography written by a young Scot, James Boswell, who adored him and suffered his moods and jibes.

In science, Isaac Newton continued to dominate men's minds for long after his death in 1727. Henry Cavendish (1730–1800), the eccentric son of the Duke of Devonshire, made some remarkable discoveries about gases and electricity but he rarely spoke of them to anyone. Joseph Black, Joseph Priestley and Sir Humphry Davy were the outstanding scientists of their age, but in medical knowledge England lagged behind the continental universities. The invention of the ship's chronometer by a watchmaker named Harrison in 1735, and the voyages of Anson and Cook, greatly increased men's knowledge of the world.

WORK

Britain forged ahead of the rest of the world through technical developments in machines, in transport and in the organisation of work. Newcomen's steam engine to pump water from mines was invented as early as 1712. This was not an efficient machine, but it was a profoundly important invention. James Watt realised its faults, and by 1781 Boulton and Watt had succeeded in producing an engine with a rotary movement to provide power for machines that had previously relied upon water power or human muscle.

The cloth-making industry had long been using machines, and relatively large numbers of workers were employed together in mills. Kay's Flying Shuttle was invented in 1733, and there followed a leap-frog race between spinners and weavers as each craft tried to keep up with the other. Arkwright's water-frame (1769), Hargreaves' Spinning Jenny and Crompton's Mule (1779) brought prosperity to the textile trade that increased as steam-power began to be applied to the machinery.

Cheap and efficient production of iron was the key to Britain's success in war and industry, and the greatest ironmaster of all was John " Iron Mad " Wilkinson who produced railroads for mines, the first iron bridge, the first iron boats and was finally buried in an iron coffin.

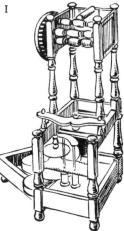

ARKWRIGHT'S
SPINNING
MACHINE

Men like Wilkinson and Wedgwood, the potter, needed better transport for their booming enterprises. Smoother roads were gradually provided by the Turnpike Trusts, until the country had an efficient and reasonably fast service of stage coaches. Even so, the roads could not carry heavy loads of coal and iron. When James Brindley, working for the Duke of Bridgewater, built the Worsley Canal (1761), the price of coal in Manchester dropped by half, and within a few years a network of canals was constructed to link the navigable rivers of Britain. By the end of the century, Trevithick had almost completed the first steam carriage that ever drew passengers, and George Stephenson, a young man of nineteen, was earning himself a local reputation for his skill with engines.

Roads and canals

Thus, unrealised by Parson Woodforde in

JAMES WATT'S HOUSE
IN GLASGOW

A MILK
STRAINER

A GRID IRON

Workers

his Norfolk rectory, Britain was already an industrial nation. In the North and in the Midlands the great factory towns were still largely unbuilt, but wherever a coal-mine or iron-works existed, or where a mill had been built because a fast-running stream supplied its power, there grew up an industrial area. The grim rows of workers' cottages made a slum village around the pit or mill, whose owner usually owned the houses, the pub and the shop as well.

In the factory, or mill, the worker's life was hard and bitter. Dependent on his master for job and home, he knew no freedom and he worked appalling hours, fourteen and sixteen hours a day for six days a week all the year, except for Christmas Day and Good Friday. Yet he could barely keep his wife and family from want. Partly because of the wars, food was dear but wages were low, since workers, especially children, were plentiful. The employers were not a class of wealthy tyrants ; many were small men, former workers, who by luck, ambition and grinding effort, had been able to set up a workshop in backyard or outhouse. Conditions and insecurity in these small-scale works were probably worse than in the barrack-like factories, because the small employers, desperate for capital and survival, were notorious for their harshness.

GRIM ROWS OF WORKERS' COTTAGES

Fear of unemployment, sickness and old age haunted the workers. Their employer rarely felt, or could afford to feel, responsible for such natural disasters, and the State provided only Poor Relief and the workhouse. But it must not be thought that the workers accepted their lot with meek resignation. They were tough, mis-shapen, brutal ; their pleasures were drink and blood-sports, and from time to time they burst out against the system that oppressed them, smashing the machines and burning down the factories.

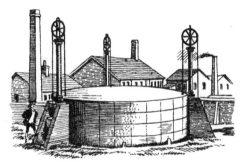

MURDOCH'S GAS HOLDER AT SOHO, BIRMINGHAM

But the picture was not wholly black. Health in the towns was better than it had been for centuries. Various Commissions for paving, for street-lighting and improvements made the towns cleaner and healthier. Cheap and more abundant clothing, especially of cotton that could be easily washed, piped water, pottery instead of pewter, hospitals and improvements in medicine all helped to reduce the death-rate. Even the factory-worker with his low wages ate better and more regularly than the country labourer and town pauper had done in days of periodic famine.

Progress

An increase in population meant an increase in the numbers of child workers, and it was only exceptional people like Jonas Hanway and Thomas Coram who were roused to anger by the knowledge that thousands of English children toiled in the pit and the factory when they should have been in the schoolroom or at play. Nevertheless, some of the increasing wealth of England did find its way downwards. There were more people of a middling sort, skilled artisans, shopkeepers and small-scale employers, more work-people receiving regular wages, even if these were supplemented by the children's hard-earned pence. The poor were very numerous, but their condition

Increase in national wealth

A TORCH
EXTINGUISHER

A SEDAN CHAIR

AN IRON DOOR-
KNOCKER

A BOOTMAKER'S
SIGN

was not quite desperate. The greatest bar to progress was the fixed belief that poverty was part of the natural state of things.

LONDON

" No, Sir," said Doctor Johnson, " when a man is tired of London he is tired of life." In the Doctor's day, even more than in ours, the commerce, arts and sciences of the kingdom were centred in the capital.

As always, London was overcrowded and was growing bigger yearly, as it swallowed up the fields and gardens that had once produced food for the swarming population. The squalor of the slums around Drury Lane and St. Giles, at Southwark and Clerkenwell was worse than ever, but elsewhere the face of London was improving. In 1757 London Bridge was cleared of its ramshackle houses, and by 1769 there were two more bridges across the river, at Blackfriars and Westminster. In the west, splendid houses were going up in places like Hanover and Cavendish Squares ; crescents, and fine streets like Albemarle, Dover and Bond Street were built off Piccadilly, and here, as in the City, where bankers, shopkeepers and merchants still lived, paving stones were put down instead of cobbles, water pipes were laid under the pavements, and lead pipes with cisterns were installed inside the houses.

Garbage and filth were carted away, and the open gutters down the middle of the streets were done away with. Unfortunately, the widespread use of water-closets caused pollution of the Thames and a return of typhoid, since the river still provided most of London's drinking water. Hanging signs were removed from shops, streets were given names and houses began to be numbered. In 1760 all the ancient gates of the City, except Temple Bar, were taken down because they hindered traffic, and street-lighting, at first only from sunset until midnight, had to be paid for by householders.

The improvements made London the finest and cleanest city in Europe. Foreigners were astonished by the splendid shops of Cheapside, the Strand and Pall Mall, where the windows were lit at night by dozens of candles : " in Oxford Road [Oxford Street] alone," declared a visitor, " there are more lamps than in the city of Paris ".

London seethed with noisy life and vigour. The riff-raff now went to enjoy themselves at the Bear-Garden at Hockley-in-the-hole, Clerkenwell, instead of crossing to Bankside as in Shakespeare's time. But they still revelled in the same blood-thirsty sports of cock-fighting, bull- and bear-baiting, and in brutal entertainments like sword-matches and boxing-matches between women. Though there were no more be-headings on Tower Hill after the '45, everyone turned out to see the hangings at Tyburn or outside Newgate Prison, when, having cheered or pelted the criminals on their last journey, a vast boisterous crowd would " see them off " with loud huzzas.

It was a cheerful, brutal age. On May Days the chimney-sweeps and milkmaids danced in the streets

A NEWS VENDOR

HOGARTH'S
DRAWING
OF THE ROUTE
TO TYBURN

DANCING ROUND
A MAYPOLE ON
MAY DAY

to the music of fiddles, and called on their customers for rewards. It was traditional for the milkmaids, the young women who sold milk from open pails, to deck themselves with ribbons and flowers and to carry on their heads, instead of the usual pail, a tray piled with jugs, tankards and coffee-pots. The coachmen and the sedan chair-men decked their vehicles, and made a parade with the butchers, link-boys, street-porters and coal-heavers, while the watermen made a rowdy procession on the river.

An established custom was for watermen and their less sedate passengers to bawl insults at every passing boat, especially if it contained well-dressed citizens. But the rudeness of the watermen was hardly worse than the behaviour of the London crowd, especially on public holidays. A foreigner noted that " it is almost dangerous for a honest man, and more particularly for a foreigner, if at all well-dressed, to walk the streets. . . . He is sure of not only being jeered at and being bespattered with mud, but as likely as not, dead dogs and cats will be thrown at him, for the mob makes a provision beforehand of these playthings."

The noise of London was tremendous. Life was rowdy, and many people lived almost wholly in the streets because their homes were no more than sleeping-dens. To the trade-cries of sweeps, coalmen, milkmaids, newsmen, knife-grinders, and a hundred more street-sellers, each with his particular call, were added the clatter of iron-rimmed wheels and the curses of chairmen and porters trying to make their way along the narrow streets. Everyone bawled at the top of his voice and was ready in a moment to put down his load or leap from his coach to finish an argument with his fists.

116

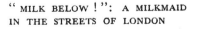

" MILK BELOW ! ": A MILKMAID
IN THE STREETS OF LONDON

As in all great cities, crime was rife, with pick-pockets everywhere and thieves plying their trade wherever people gathered for business or pleasure. There was no regular police force, only the Parish Constables and the Watch who patrolled the streets at night crying the hour. But, from feebleness or dishonesty, they did little to protect honest citizens. From time to time the danger from regular criminals was increased by the activities of hooligans like the Mohocks. These gangs roamed the streets looking for " sport " that varied from tying up door-knockers to actual murder. Inoffensive persons going home late were likely to be set upon for no reason, their coach or sedan-chair overturned, their eyes blackened and their clothes ruined. Jonathan Swift more than once noted, " I came home in a chair for fear of the Mohocks," though he realised that the mere sight of a sedan-chair at night could invite attack, and he added, " Lord Winchelsea told me . . . that two of the Mohocks caught a maid of old Lady Winchelsea's . . . they cut all her face and beat her without any provocation . . . one of those taken [i.e. arrested] is a baronet."

The magistrates, the parish constables and a handful of doddering watchmen could not control London's crime. The wonder was that it was not worse. When riots occurred, and they were always likely to flare up at any excuse, the soldiers were called out, but by that time, a great deal of damage and often loss of life had occurred.* Moreover, Englishmen detested soldiers, and their very appearance sometimes led to greater violence.

* As late as 1780 occurred the *Gordon Riots*. Parliament had passed an Act abolishing some of the severer penalties against Roman Catholics, and a mob, led by the insane Lord Gordon, marched to the House of Commons to protest. Rioting broke out, houses were sacked and the Newgate prison was burned down and its prisoners released. The mob terrorised London for several days until the Army restored order, and some of the leaders were executed.

A RUSHLIGHT
HOLDER

A STEW POT

A BOOT-CLEANING
JACK

Crime

Magistrates tried offering rewards for the capture of thieves, but this caused rogues to tempt youngsters into crime in order to win rewards for informing on them. Jonathan Wild was a celebrated villain who made a fortune from his " thief-taking " ; he also arranged robberies, received the stolen goods and sold them back to the owners under a cloak of respectability, until he was unmasked and executed in 1725. " Trading justices " took bribes from men like Wild, and sold justice to the highest bidders, until Henry Fielding and his brother Sir John, " the blind Beak ", began to introduce respect for the law.

The Fieldings were paid magistrates at Bow Street where they organised a body of reliable men to arrest footpads and track down robbers. These officers in their red waistcoats became known as " Robin Redbreasts " and, later, as Bow Street Runners. In 1783 the Treasury paid for a Police Horse Patrol to safeguard the roads into London, and this so reduced highway robbery that the Patrol was soon abolished. Naturally, the robbers came back again, but the usefulness of a regular police force had been proved. The greatest obstacle to reform was the obstinate belief that a strong police force would be an outrage to the liberties of freeborn Englishmen.

A BOW STREET
RUNNER

At this time, prisons were looked on not as places of punishment but as temporary lodgings, from which debtors could free themselves by paying up, and from which criminals were removed to the gallows or to the convict ships that regularly sailed to the West Indies and the American colonies. Thus, jailers charged for board and lodging and made a fat profit.

Prisons

In 1729 the post of Warden of the Fleet Prison was sold for £5000, and there were many privately owned jails in the country whose keepers made a comfortable living. A debtor or a prisoner awaiting trial had to buy his own food and drink, for the official rations

CONVICT SHIPS
WERE KNOWN AS
PRISON HULKS

were only for convicted felons. If he had money, a prisoner could live well, have a private room, his servant and his friends to visit him, but if he was penniless he had to exist by selling the clothes off his back or by begging from visitors. Sometimes prisoners, chained together, were led outside to beg in the streets. Even if he was acquitted by the court, a man could not go free until he had paid the " garnish money " for being let out.

Foreigners considered London to be " the wickedest city in the world ", and were horrified by its punishment of wrong-doers. In George III's reign, there were nearly two hundred offences which could be punished by death ; but such savagery only increased crime, because if a man could hang for stealing a watch, he might as well kill its owner to avoid being recognised later. If the theft of property worth five shillings could bring a boy or a starving woman to the gallows, the owner, in order to save a life, might well say the property was worth less, or a jury might refuse to bring in a verdict of " guilty ". *Savage punishments*

Though punishment was savage, pity was not entirely absent. Men like John Howard did their utmost to awaken the public to the horrors of prison life, and the work was carried on by Elizabeth Fry who came

119

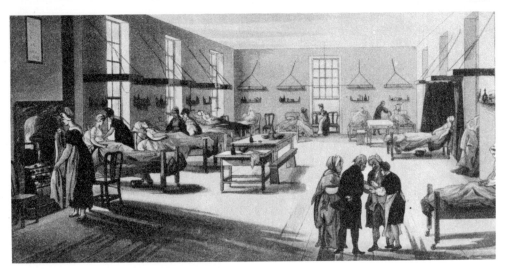

A WARD IN THE MIDDLESEX HOSPITAL

Hospitals

to London in 1800. Many of the great hospitals were founded during the 18th century, the Westminster, St George's and the London ; Guy's in 1724 and the Middlesex in 1745. There was a Maternity (or Lying-in) Hospital for poor women, and the famous Foundling Hospital, built by public subscription through the efforts of a sailor, Captain Coram, for infants who were so often found abandoned in alleys and porches.

Greenwich Hospital, a superb building, provided shelter for wounded sailors, and in the country there were hundreds of almshouses and charity schools built by private persons. Bedlam, the lunatic-asylum, was one of the sights of London where visitors went to be amused by the antics of madmen who were exhibited in cages like wild animals. It was also the custom, equally horrifying, for people of every class to look in at Bridewell to see women prisoners *Bridewell* being whipped for their wrong-doing, and to watch them beating flax with a mallet under the savage eye of Captain " Whip 'em ", the overseer.

The fashionable world still paraded in the Mall, though they complained that a commoner sort of person had taken to walking there on Sundays. The covered piazza at Covent Garden was thronged with gallants who ogled the shop-girls and maidservants, while the New Spring Gardens (later known as Vauxhall Gardens) and Ranelagh were favourite promenades on summer evenings. The gardens were laid out with lawns, hedges and gravel-walks, with little pavilions here and there, where tea was served, as well as chocolate, punch, arrack and a liqueur called ratafia. Acrobats, singers and balloonists provided entertainment, and there was always the chance of a raid by the Press Gang to add to the evening's excitement. At the Tower there were the Crown Jewels to be seen, as well as suits of armour and the wild beasts. There was the British Museum, opened in 1757, another museum in Leicester Square, Mrs. Salmon's Wax-works in Fleet Street, and the royal parks where cows and red deer browsed as the coaches went by.

Fashionable entertainment

This was the century of the coffee-house and the chop-house. Coffee-houses were particularly numerous in the neighbourhood of Drury Lane, Covent Garden and the Royal Exchange, and most of them, like public-houses in later times, had their regular customers. Tories went to the Cocoa-Tree and Orsinda's, Whigs gathered at the Coffee-house of St. James's, writers were to be found at Old Slaughter's unless they were listening to Doctor Johnson at the Bedford or the Turk's Head. There were coffee-houses favoured by stockbrokers, by Army officers and

Coffee-houses

DOCTOR JOHNSON
IN A COFFEE-
HOUSE

ST. JAMES'S STREET IN 1800, SHOWING BOODLE'S CLUB (LEFT)
AND BROOKS'S CLUB (RIGHT)

booksellers ; at Lloyd's in Lombard Street merchants and sea-captains gathered to hear shipping news read out by a serving-boy, and to arrange insurance on cargo and vessels. At the better houses newspapers, pens, ink and writing-paper were provided, and in some cases music and dice, but the chief attractions of the coffee-house were the company, the talk and the news.

The aristocratic world soon founded its own exclusive version of the coffee-house. For a subscription of from about five to ten guineas a year, the wealthy man-about-town could meet his acquaintances to dine, gossip and play cards at his club. The most famous of the London clubs were Brooks's, Crockford's, White's and Almack's in St. James's. The passion for betting was as deep-seated as it was reckless. Men would bet on their horses and dogs, on a race between footmen or servant-girls. They would wager large

Gambling

sums on a duel or an eating-match, for no contest was too absurd and no stakes too high. It was said that a man could sit down at the card-table at White's after dinner and go to bed about dawn ruined, his house, estate, carriages, his wife's fortune and his son's inheritance all lost in a game of cards.

122

SPAS

The wealthy classes gambled, ate and drank too much because most of them had too little to do. Servants were cheap, and any kind of exertion, except for pleasure, was despised by rich and poor alike. In order to pass the time agreeably and to correct the effects of over-eating and over-drinking, it became customary for fashionable people, with their imitators and hangers-on, to visit a spa for a few weeks of the year.

Bath, famous for its hot springs since Roman times, had fallen into decay and was of little account until Beau Nash went there in 1702. Nash, an extravagant dandy who lived by gambling, transformed the city and became, as Master of Ceremonies, its unchallenged ruler throughout the greater part of the reigns of Queen Anne and the first two Georges. He not only engaged an orchestra to play to those who came to drink the waters, but he organised an Assembly Room, borrowed money to pave the streets and witnessed the erection of the most gracious buildings of his time. Nash also imposed a set of rules which transformed the manners of the upper classes. Dirt and disorder were banished ; swearing, quarrelling and the carrying of swords were forbidden, so that ladies could venture out of doors without an escort. Visitors arriving at Bath were greeted by liveried footmen who showed them to a suite at the " White Hart ", lit by candles and warmed by a blazing fire. At the balls and assemblies a code of elegant behaviour was insisted upon and late hours were never permitted, even at the gaming-tables, where Nash himself took a percentage of the winnings.

The daily routine began with a visit to one of the baths. Men and women waded about up to their necks in the lukewarm water, exchanging greetings

Beau Nash transforms Bath

A DANDY

with the spectators. Ladies wore vast bathing cos-
tumes and often pushed in front of them little floating
trays holding handkerchief, sweets and snuff-box. As
the bathers rose from the water, attendants wrapped
them in blankets and carried them to sedan chairs to
be taken back to their apartments. Next came the
drinking of the waters in the Pump Room ; then
breakfast in the Assembly Rooms, followed by Divine
Service at church. The rest of the day was passed in
strolling about the gardens, visiting acquaintances,
the shops and the library, and the evening was spent
at the ball, the theatre or the gaming-table. Beau
Nash supervised every aspect of life at Bath, acting as
Master of Ceremonies with the utmost strictness.
Once when Princess Amelia, George II's daughter,
asked for one more dance after eleven o'clock, Nash
replied, " Madam, *I* am king here and my laws must
be kept ! "

There were well-known spas at Harrogate, Buxton,
Cheltenham and Tunbridge Wells, which was second
only to Bath in elegance. The spa at Epsom declined
when horse-racing became popular there, for the
race-course toughs soon drove out the genteel visitors.
Hampstead, a village just north of London, and
Richmond were small spas near the capital which
attracted shopkeepers, business people and some less
desirable folk.

The success of the spas led to an interest in seaside
towns, or " watering-places " as they were called.

BATHING AT
BRIGHTON

Doctors began to recommend sea-bathing and even the drinking of sea-water, so that by 1750 there were " bathing-machines " at Margate. In George III's reign, his son, " Prinny " the Prince of Wales, took such a fancy to Brighton that it quickly became a fashionable resort with handsome terraces and the bizarre Pavilion. Another

ON BOARD SHIP

century was to pass, however, before ordinary citizens regarded sea-bathing as anything more than a weird fad.

NAVY AND ARMY

Doctor Johnson once remarked to Boswell, " A ship is worse than a jail. There is, in a jail, better air, better company, better conveniency of every kind ; and a ship has the additional disadvantage of being in danger."

During the 18th century the British became the greatest seafaring nation in the world. The national wealth depended largely upon the merchant fleets, and the country's safety depended upon the Navy. Yet, as Johnson said, the ships were worse than prisons and the seamen were treated like felons. So harsh were conditions on board that the Navy could not have put to sea if its crews had not been completed by desperate fellows who volunteered in order to escape from crime or debt, and by the unfortunate wretches who were swept up by the Press Gang.

" A ship is worse than a jail "

Seamen were paid only 19 to 24 shillings a month, and this pay, from which all kinds of deductions could

125

Seamen's pay

be made, was not due until the ship returned to England. Even then, naval pay was frequently in arrears because the Government had not granted the necessary funds to the Naval Pay Office. It was true that sailors could also earn prize money through the capture of enemy ships, but the method of sharing was amazingly unjust. When Havana in the West Indies was captured in 1762, the Admiral received over £100,000, captains about £1,600 each, petty officers £17 and seamen £3 14s. 9½d. apiece.

The Press Gang was the legal method of raising men in time of war, and it usually operated in and about seafaring towns where almost any man was likely to have some acquaintance with the sea. Particularly harsh was the practice of boarding coastal vessels in harbour and merchant ships on their way home up the Channel. After three or four years in Indian waters and within sight of Dover, a seaman who was longing to see his family would find himself hustled on board one of His Majesty's warships to serve for as long as the war lasted. At times, when men were needed desperately, the Press Gang had to work inland. West Country towns like Gloucester were raided, and when James Watt was studying as a young man in London in 1754, he dared not go out for fear of being " taken ". Naval commanders disliked these inland raids, for they complained that clerks and tailors were of no use afloat, being " poor little sickly fellows ".

AN INLAND RAID
BY THE PRESS
GANG

The shocking conditions of service in the Navy were not caused by brutal officers, but by Parliament's neglect of the Service until it had a war on its hands. Senior officers usually sympathised with the men's grievances and often spoke up for them. " Our fleets are defrauded by injustice, manned by violence and maintained by cruelty," declared Admiral Vernon.

But, at sea, discipline had to be iron-hard, when the safety of the ship and of the nation depended upon absolute obedience. In a brutal age, twenty-four lashes upon a man's back (the maximum that could be awarded) was no worse a punishment than could be expected ashore. A boatswain had to be ready with his fists to keep order among ruffians, and no one expected anything except hard conditions, bad food and constant danger. What did cause bitter resentment, apart from pay arrears, was the custom of refusing shore-leave when a ship was in home waters and the men were in sight of taverns and girls. But the captain who knew that half his men would desert if once they set foot ashore, dared not grant the leave that he knew was well deserved.

Fortunately, the Navy was well-officered, since the old system of promoting Court gentlemen above the heads of " tarpaulin captains " had died out. Boys from middle-class homes went to sea at 12 to 14 years of age, usually as volunteers without pay in the charge of a captain who was probably known to their families ; young Nelson, for instance, the son of a clergyman, went as " captain's servant " to his uncle, Captain Suckling. These youngsters served for six or seven years as able seamen and midshipmen, until they became 3rd lieutenants after a stiff examination by a board of officers. Thereafter, promotion depended partly on merit, but chiefly on influence. Reliable officers might never rise above a lieutenant's rank, yet

The training of Naval officers

Nelson was captain of his own ship before he was twenty-one because, in addition to brilliant ability, he had an uncle who by then was Comptroller of the Navy. Promotion to the highest ranks, however, was by seniority, and it was common for admirals to keep their posts until well past the age of 70 ; Sir John Morris, Admiral of the Fleet in 1744, was called upon to repel a major invasion when he was 84.

There was no official uniform in the Navy. Seamen usually wore red breeches, grey jackets and striped waistcoats, for which a deduction was made from their pay, and officers wore what they pleased until George II introduced a standard uniform in 1748. As for food, rascally contractors made fortunes out of supplying rations that were frequently unfit to eat before a ship left harbour, but, in any case, there was no way of keeping food in good condition, apart from salting or pickling the meat. Flour for bread-making quickly deteriorated at sea, and Englishmen despised fruit and vegetables even when they were available. As a result, scurvy was a killing disease on long voyages and in the West Indies, where many ships saw years of service. In the first year of Anson's voyage round the world, he lost 626 of his 961 men, nearly all from disease, but Captain Cook, having suffered losses almost as disastrous during his first great voyage, forced his reluctant crews to vary their meat and biscuits diet with fruit and vegetables. This measure, with less alcohol and greater cleanliness below decks, wrought a miracle, for only one man out of 118 died from sickness during the three-year cruise of the *Resolution* in 1772–75.

At the end of the century, conditions in the Navy led to the two mutinies that deeply shocked a nation proud of its sailors, even if it half-starved them. Anson had made some reforms forty years before, by obtaining prompter pay for the men, with the right to

Scurvy

CAPTAIN COOK

set aside money for their wives, but Navy administration remained shockingly lax and confused. In 1797, when England was struggling against revolutionary France, the Fleet at Spithead (off Portsmouth) refused to sail. Pay had not been raised since Charles II's reign, provisions were as bad as ever, pensions were miserably small (a year's pay was all that a widow received) and wounded pay had been reduced.

SAILORS COMPLAINING OF THEIR RATIONS BEFORE THE MUTINY

The mutineers kept discipline marvellously well and, as soon as a few unpopular officers had been removed and the government had given some sort of promise about pay, they asked to be allowed to get to grips with the enemy.

More serious was the mutiny at the Nore, where the North Sea fleet was anchored at the mouth of the Thames. Led by Richard Parker, a seaman of some education, the sailors were in a much more dangerous mood. They blockaded the river, threatened London with famine, and made such unreasonable demands that the Government refused to give way. There was little sympathy ashore for the mutineers or from the Spithead men. Nearly all the sailors soon came to their senses and returned to the authority of their officers: Parker and a few ring-leaders were hanged. The rest of the ex-mutineers, sent into action to aid Admiral Duncan, who had been bluffing the Dutch with only three ships, made such efforts to prove their loyalty that, at the *Battle of Camperdown*, the Dutch Navy was destroyed.

Mutiny at the Nore 1797

THE " VICTORY "

The spirit of the Navy

The mutinies drew attention to the hardships suffered by the sailors on whom England depended for her very survival. The worst of the grievances were met, and conditions in the service gradually improved. Officers like Anson, Cook, Vernon and Nelson had inspired in their rough seamen a devotion and rugged courage that were nothing short of miraculous. It was in them and in the tradition they forged that England's naval superiority lay. These were the men who, in a dozen major actions, roared out their choruses as the ships moved steadily into the enemy's midst, suffered the horrors of grape-shot and naval surgery, huzza'ed as they went alongside the enemy, and still could weep for the admiral who died on the *Victory* alongside their mates.

The Army

If the Navy was usually neglected, it was at least regarded with affectionate pride, but the Army was heartily disliked. Englishmen distrusted armed forces and begrudged every penny that was spent on their upkeep. Thus, in war-time, new regiments had to be raised hastily and for the shortest terms possible. The ranks were filled from the jails and the poorhouses, and by the activities of the " Crimp ", the equivalent of the Press Gang, but when the war ended, the Army was allowed to shrink back into weakness.

The regular forces were small ; Marlborough had no more than about 18,000 British troops in 1702 ; and in 1739, the national army totalled some 36,000, compared with 130,000 Spaniards and 300,000 Frenchmen.   Even in 1812, during the Napoleonic wars, when the Army won popularity for a time, Britain had only 145,000 troops overseas with 60,000 hired foreigners, and about 250,000 militiamen at home, from a population of at least eleven millions.   Between the triumphs of our two greatest soldiers, Marlborough, early in the century, and Wellington at its end, any crisis or outbreak of war found the Army small, inefficient and corrupt.   Irish, Dutch, Hanoverian or German troops had to be hired to stave off disaster, and even to settle domestic troubles like the Jacobite rebellions.

A FOOT-SOLDIER

Unlike the revolutionary armies of France and our armed Services today, the British Army in the 18th century was not drawn from the civilian population as a whole.   The officers came from aristocratic and wealthy families, while the troops were taken from the lowest classes of society ; in Wellington's famous words, his soldiers were " the scum of the earth ", though he added, " it is really wonderful that we should have made them the fine fellows they are ".

" *the scum of the earth* "

A man who enlisted as a private soldier had usually sunk about as low as he could go.   Drink, unemployment, debt, or some trouble at home caused him to accept the King's money from a recruiting-sergeant in an ale-house.   By morning, he found himself a soldier in the ranks, subject to iron discipline, brutal treatment and the lash.   His pay was sixpence a day, his food poor and drink all too plentiful.   At home, he would be shunned by decent folk, and no respectable girl would walk out with a soldier.   Abroad, he would be far more likely to die from camp

NAVAL OFFICERS CAME
FROM WEALTHY FAMILIES

The infantryman

fever than by enemy bullets, especially if sent to serve on garrison duty in the West Indies, which was well-nigh a death sentence. On campaign, he would see his officers living in luxury, transported by carriages or on horseback, while he trudged on foot, carrying his pack and hauling the guns through North American woods or across the Spanish plains. But if he survived, he was indeed a soldier. Stubborn, wonderfully disciplined, never knowing when they were defeated, Wellington's infantry were the finest in the world.

Officers' commissions were bought at high prices, often for mere boys, and officers recouped the heavy cost at the expense of the men or from the pay of non-existent soldiers supposedly on the roll. A junior officer could not live on his pay and was expected to have a private income, but the colonel of a regiment who had spent lavishly to obtain his promotion, was at last in a position to make money. The regiment was looked upon as his own property and, until the middle of the century, was known by his name. He usually made a handsome income from recruiting and from the troops' food and clothing. Soldiers never forgot an officer like the Marquis of Granby, colonel of the Royal Horse Guards, who treated them well, whose name is still found on inn-signs all over England.

A GRENADIER

After the time of Marlborough—" Soldier John ", who would have no truck with playing at war—officers underwent little or no military training, for they looked on their profession as a social asset that allowed them to enjoy life and to wear splendid dress in public. Wellington had to chide his officers for putting up umbrellas on the battlefield, and men like Pitt and Wolfe who made a study of military tactics, were considered odd to say the least. The training of the men was controlled by the sergeants, for some

Dandified officers

officers simply absented themselves from duty whenever they chose and, even on campaign, went home if they pleased. In battle, they were generally brave enough, but few had studied their profession and some, like Lord George Sackville* at Minden were liable to take offence if given unwelcome orders. In such a service, officers without money or influence, no matter how capable, remained captains or lieutenants throughout their careers.

A disobedient officer

George I and George II both prided themselves on their military knowledge, and the Duke of Cumberland, commander of the British Army at the age of twenty-five, managed to improve discipline and to limit the amount of baggage that officers could take on campaign. The example of Prussian and Hanoverian troops caused drill to be overhauled and training to be improved, but, apart from a short period during the Napoleonic Wars, the Army remained unpopular and neglected.

* Though repeatedly ordered to charge, Lord Sackville refused to allow the English cavalry to do so, because he was " dis-obliged " (offended) with Prince Ferdinand of Brunswick. Pitt had his former friend court-martialled and the sentence read out to every British regiment.

PART THREE

IN THE REIGN OF GEORGE III

CHAPTER 8

THE LOSS OF THE AMERICAN COLONIES

George III decides to " be a king "

BY 1770 it seemed that George III had achieved his supreme object in life, to " be a king ". Pitt was a sick and disillusioned man after the Treaty of Paris, and the government had blundered along without him while the King built up his party of " friends " in Parliament. Outmanoeuvred, and divided among themselves, the Whigs lost influence and George felt that the time had come for him to govern the country through ministers of his own choosing.

The King was painstaking and shrewd, especially in his judgement of men's weaknesses, but he lacked the ability to take a far-sighted and tolerant view of events outside his narrow experience. For Prime Minister he chose Lord North, a man whose sole political aim was to please his master, and between them they might have established some kind of royal dictatorship had there not arisen a crisis in North America that revealed their incapacity, and almost brought disaster to their country.

The British colonies in North America had developed in different ways from various beginnings. They were independent of each other, and each had its own Charter to govern its affairs through an elected Assembly. Almost the only links with Britain, apart from race and trade, were the royal Governor, the judges and certain officials.

The colonists were rugged, tight-fisted and self-confident. They resented the officials who were sent

THE FLAG OF
THE COLONISTS

134

COLONISTS
IN NEW
ENGLAND

out and sometimes refused to pay their salaries ; they
ignored the regulations by which they were supposed
to trade only with the Mother Country and had no
feelings of gratitude towards the country that had
saved them from French domination.

After the Seven Years War, it was felt in Britain
that, since the huge cost of defending the colonies had
fallen upon the people at home, the colonies ought to
contribute something towards protecting their own
territory. Walpole, of course, had let sleeping dogs
lie, but during the late war the colonists had persist-
ently and illegally traded with the French, even to the
extent of denying stores to the British soldiers. Now
that the peace had added to the Empire vast territories
west of the Alleghany Mountains, a permanent force of
10,000 soldiers was needed to protect the settlers from
the Indians. However, the colonies were as hostile to
each other as they were to the idea of paying half the
cost of this protective force.

It is as well to look at the situation through the
colonists' eyes. There were now over two million of
them. Some were French and Germans, many were

The colonists' viewpoint

Scottish and Irish peasants who had been forced overseas because they could not gain a living at home ; the majority were of English stock, but the numbers of English immigrants had been decreasing because there was less religious and political trouble at home. Many of the colonists or, more likely, their grandfathers, had settled in America for religion's sake ; some had gone to better themselves, but far more had been thrust out of England for less worthy reasons and it was foolish to suppose that they or their children should feel loyalty towards her.

Ignorance at home

Politicians and citizens in England were extremely ignorant about colonies that were six weeks' voyage away, and it was impossible for them to visualise conditions in a land whose seaboard was over three thousand miles long, where climate and geography varied as greatly as from Scotland to West Africa. To the merchants and the ruling-class in England, the colonies were a God-given source of raw materials and a dumping ground for manufactured goods, for thieves, bankrupts and undesirables of every kind. The colonists sensed this patronising attitude in the aristocrats who arrived to take up official posts and they heartily resented it.

If the Americans were accused of smuggling and of disobedience to the Mercantile Acts, they could reply that laws forcing them to trade only with Britain were hindering their rightful development. The trade in cotton and tobacco, for instance, was controlled by English businessmen, and the planters were heavily and unfairly in debt to them. All manufactured goods

IMMIGRANTS ARRIVE
AT AN AMERICAN
PORT

were supposed to be purchased from England and this stifled the manufacturing activity that New England, in particular, was capable of developing.

The Stamp Act

When Grenville, who succeeded Bute as Prime Minister in 1763, decided that it was only reasonable for the colonies to pay a share towards their own upkeep, he tried to enforce the Navigation Acts and to suppress smuggling. In 1765 a Stamp Duty was placed on newspapers and legal documents to bring in a modest sum towards colonial defence. Not a penny would go to Britain which, alone of all colonising powers, had never squeezed money from her colonies. But, in America, furious protests were raised. The Stamp Act was repealed, but Parliament stated its right to tax the colonies if it wished. Charles Townshend, the Chancellor of the Exchequer, put customs duties at American ports on six articles—glass, paper, painters' colours, red and white lead and tea. Angry opposition caused all these to be withdrawn, except the tax on tea which was 3d. on a pound.

CHARLES
TOWNSHEND

By this time, common sense had departed. The colonists declared that they would have " No Taxation without Representation ", meaning that they would not pay taxes imposed by Parliament at Westminster where they had no Members. Yet, when the taxes were removed, they complained that the American market would be flooded by cheap goods. To help the East India Company, tea was allowed to be shipped direct to America without the normal duty at British ports, and this made tea much cheaper, even with the 3d. tax. But cheap tea was a blow at the smuggling trade and the tax was vile tyranny. On one side, the colonists seemed to forget that the tax was to help them ; on the other side, the British Government did not try to understand the colonists' point of view and their natural dislike of being given orders by a Parliament three thousand miles away.

A tax on tea

THE BOSTON
TEA PARTY

In December 1773 a party of fifty men dressed as Red Indians boarded three ships in Boston harbour and threw their cargoes of tea into the water.

The King punishes
Boston

The *Boston Tea Party* was an act of defiance, which no self-respecting government could ignore. In England, where there had been much sympathy with the colonists over the Stamp Act, it was generally felt that the insolent Bostonians should be punished. Lord North, that is to say the King, had the Customs House removed from Boston, which was equivalent to closing the port, and suspended the Charter which gave Massachusetts its right to self-government.

King George and his ministers succeeded in doing what the Indians and the French had failed to do, they caused the colonies to unite. New England, always the most active colony in every field, took the lead by inviting the rest to a Continental Congress at Philadelphia in September, 1774, at which a Declaration of Rights was drawn up, in much the same spirit as an English Parliament had stated its case to Charles I. But even at this stage no one believed that

The " Olive
Branch Petition "

a final break must come about. The Congress sent an " Olive Branch Petition " to the King, setting down their grievances but affirming their loyalty to the Crown. George, however, stung by Whig attacks

138

on Lord North's government, refused to take any notice of the Petition.

Meanwhile, in New England, the Assembly had organised a body of militia, known as " minutemen ", because they were ready to serve at a minute's notice. In April .1775 General Gage, the British Governor at Boston, sent a detachment of troops up-country to Concord, where the members of the dissolved Assembly had organised a militia and col-lected military stores. The troops had orders to des-troy or capture the stores. At *Lexington* village near Concord they were fired on by minutemen. A running attack, with sniping from cover of the woods, was kept up throughout the return march to Boston and 293 soldiers were killed. The War of American Independence had begun. *The first battle*

As tension mounted in Boston, Gage did nothing until it came to his notice that a force of " Yankees " had taken possession of *Bunker's Hill*, overlooking Boston harbour. In an action that was badly mis-managed, the British took the hill but lost 1000 men to 400 of the local citizen army. Gage was replaced by General Howe, brother of the Admiral, but these two skirmishes made a peaceful settlement well-nigh impossible. They showed that the colonists could fully hold their own with regular troops if they used their knowledge of the countryside.

At Philadelphia, the Congress of the United Colonies appointed George Washington to be Com-mander-in-Chief of its " Continental Army ". No better choice could have been made, for Washington had served under Braddock in the Seven Years War, so he not only had experience as an officer, but he understood the strength and weakness of the volunteer army which he commanded.

The colonies were still united in name only. Jeal-ousy divided them, and meanness kept Washington

GEORGE
WASHINGTON

short of munitions and stores. Most of the militiamen refused to serve outside their own states and desertions, even acts of treachery, were not unusual in an army where privates considered themselves as good as their officers and many of the officers were jealous of their commander.

Canada stands firm

However, taking the offensive during the winter of 1775, Congress ordered an attack on Canada by an expedition under Benedict Arnold and Montgomery. This was a complete failure, for Quebec stood firm. It might have been expected that the French-Canadians would side with the rebellious Americans, but Lord North's Quebec Act (1774) had given a large measure of self-government and freedom to the Roman Catholics. Thus Canada remained loyal to Britain.

In the spring of 1776 Washington tried manfully to inject some discipline into his motley army and he prepared to attack Boston, where General Howe showed no more energy than Gage. The British command seemed to take the view that the best plan was to sit still and do nothing. The colonists, it was thought, would soon collapse from lack of money, stores and military experience, and their internal jealousies would rapidly bring the rebellion to an end. Severe action by the British might delay this collapse and lead to lasting bitterness but, in fact, time was to prove America's best ally.

Washington's task

For the moment, the colonists' task appeared hopeless, for their ill-equipped forces were opposed by regular troops, many of whom had seen service on European battlefields. The rebels had no artillery, no trained body of officers, no navy and no financial resources to meet the cost of a long war. Their only advantages seemed to lie in their knowledge of their huge country, in their aptitude for guerilla warfare, and in the character of Washington, whose patient

THE BATTLE OF LEXINGTON, THE FIRST
ACTION OF THE WAR OF INDEPENDENCE

fortitude upheld his countrymen through every trial
and disaster.

It is scarcely possible to doubt that an intelligent
and energetic commander would have suppressed the
colonists within a year. But Howe feebly withdrew
his troops from Boston to Long Island and took possession of New York whose inhabitants greeted the British
with enthusiasm. The British fleet, which could have
blockaded the American ports and brought their
shipping to a standstill, remained at anchor in New
York harbour. Later, it became clear that both the
Army and the fleet were too small for the work which
they had been given. There were no plans, no decisive
blows, no evidence of Britain's might, apart from a *Inactivity by*
naval squadron and a miscellaneous force of 30,000 *the British*
men including German hired troops, whose presence
gave particular offence to the Americans. It seemed
unnecessarily barbarous to bring foreign mercenaries,
who were notorious for their brutality, into what was
still regarded as a domestic squabble.

By the summer of 1776, instead of being engaged in
a desperate struggle against hopeless odds, Congress
was able to meet at Philadelphia, defiant and confident.

The Declaration of Independence, July 4th 1776

On July 4th the delegates signed the famous Declaration of Independence, which included the celebrated statements, " that all men are created equal ; that they are endowed by their Creator with certain inalienable rights ; that among these are life, liberty and the pursuit of happiness ". The situation was now quite different from 1773. As usually happens in a conflict of this kind, the extremists had taken charge and a quarrel among British citizens had become a war for independence.

Meanwhile, Washington moved south and tried to drive the British from Long Island, but in a battle at *Brooklyn*, the colonial troops were beaten by the regulars. With great difficulty Washington extricated his army and retreated across New Jersey to Philadelphia. His soldiers were in poor shape and if Howe had struck hard, the Continental Army must have been broken. But the British commander did nothing for the rest of the year.

It must be doubted whether conquest was possible. The Americans could have been crushed in the field and perhaps forced to make some kind of surrender, but their grievances would have been more bitter than ever, and revolt would have flared up again at the earliest opportunity. Thus, the British government failed doubly. They, and the nation as a whole, had failed to think out the relationship between a Mother Country and her colonies, and, when war unhappily broke out, they failed to conduct it with the vigour that was necessary to end it quickly.

Having survived the first phase, the American cause began to prosper. Washington's raw recruits gained in confidence and experience with every month that passed, for as Chatham said later, three years were spent " in teaching the American show to fight ". American ships began to prey on British merchantmen and, in

INDEPENDENCE HALL, PHILADELPHIA (WHERE THE DECLARATION OF INDEPENDENCE WAS SIGNED)

Paris, Benjamin Franklin was winning unofficial support in the form of stores and money.

In 1777 King George and his advisers had a master plan to cut off New England, core of the resistance, from the rest of the colonies. General Burgoyne was to advance from Canada down the Hudson Valley, while Howe was to move up from New York to meet him. Unfortunately, the orders were sufficiently vague to allow Howe to conduct a sideshow of his own. He decided that he would first finish off the main American army, so he advanced to Philadelphia and defeated Washington at *Brandywine*. But he had undertaken the campaign too late in the year and too late for poor Burgoyne who had already set out from Canada. Attacked all the way by guerilla troops, Burgoyne's redcoats could only trudge on through trackless wooded country, hoping for relief that never came. Eventually, outnumbered and completely surrounded by an enemy that did not understand the European way of fighting battles, Burgoyne's army of 8000 men laid down their arms at *Saratoga Springs* (October 1777).

Washington's defeat was completely unimportant compared with the effect of Burgoyne's surrender.

BENJAMIN FRANKLIN

Surrender at Saratoga

BURGOYNE'S SURRENDER AT SARATOGA SPRINGS

The effect of
Saratoga Springs

The loss of 8000 men could have been easily repaired, but Saratoga won the war for the colonists because it convinced England's enemies that America now had a chance of victory.   In February 1778 France entered the war and Spain soon followed suit.   Both countries naturally wanted to avenge the losses of the Seven Years War and were only too ready to take sides against their old enemy ; it was ironic that two despotic governments which allowed their own colonies no freedom whatever, should become champions of independence.

The combined French and Spanish fleets outnumbered the British, and command of the sea was lost when Holland also joined the French.   Worse followed when Prussia, Sweden, Russia and Denmark formed the *League of Armed Neutrality* (1780) to resist the British Navy's practice of searching neutral ships that might be carrying goods to America.   The League was the work of Frederick the Great, who thus took his revenge for being deserted by Britain when George III put an end to the Seven Years War.   Had Frederick as much as hinted that he would support Britain, not a single soldier would have been moved from France to America, but Frederick forgot the help that Pitt gave to Prussia and only remembered being left in the lurch by George III.

Britain at war
with France, Spain
and Holland

Faced with this array of enemies, Britain's best hope lay in preventing aid from reaching America, while an all-out drive put an end to the fighting there, but George and his ministers were incapable of such energetic ruthlessness.   The Navy was scattered about the world so that an effective blockade of French and Spanish ports was impossible.   British merchantmen were attacked at sea and even off our own coasts, until 3000 ships were lost.   An enemy fleet cruised in the Channel and actually anchored in Falmouth Bay. Minorca and Gibraltar were besieged, West Indian islands were lost, and the Spaniards captured Florida and the Bahamas. In India, France threatened to break the power of the East India Company by aiding an alliance of Mahratta princes.

Despite these embarrassments, it seemed for the moment as if the American campaign might be brought to an end by securing the South and then, aided by its " loyalist " regiments, concentrating all the British forces against George Washington. General Cornwallis advanced from Charleston to overrun Virginia and Pennsylvania. After that, he was to join with General Clinton who would move from New York so that Washington could be crushed.

Loss of sea-power defeated the plan. A well-equipped French force under La Fayette was able to land and to prevent Clinton from leaving New York. Cornwallis was therefore ordered to retire to York-town Peninsula with his back to the sea, from which the British fleet would support and supply his army. Eight days later there arrived off the coast a French fleet that was too powerful for the British admiral to dislodge. The result was the exact reverse of the original plan. Instead of being threatened by two forces, Washington was able to move the whole American army to seal off the peninsula. Hemmed in by land and sea, Cornwallis made gallant efforts to get out of the trap, but he had to surrender at *Yorktown* in October 1781.

Surrender at Yorktown

When Lord North heard the news of the disaster he exclaimed, " O God ! It is all over ! " The fighting in America was ended, but Britain still had to carry on the war against three European powers. North resigned and the Whigs under Rockingham took over the government. They had constantly proclaimed the justice of the colonists' claims, but, like the whole nation, they were in no mood to yield to France and Spain.

ENG. BK. III—10

Victory at sea

In the end Britain came off less badly than might have been expected, for Admiral Rodney defeated the Franco-Spanish fleet in the West Indies in a brilliant victory near some tiny islands called " *The Saints* " (1782), and this recovery re-established the belief that the British were invincible at sea. Minorca had been lost, but Gibraltar, where Sir George Eliott held out stubbornly for over two years, was finally relieved by Admiral Lord Howe. In India, Warren Hastings and Eyre Coote survived all their difficulties and thwarted the French plans.

Thus, when the Treaty of Versailles ended the war in 1783, Britain had saved some shreds of pride and her losses were not so great as they might have been. The 13 American colonies, of course, gained complete independence, though there was not yet any notion of a united country stretching from Atlantic to the Pacific. A line passing through the Great Lakes to the Mississippi basin marked the new republic's western boundary, for France retained Louisiana. Canada, thanks to the Quebec Act, remained in the Empire. The colonists in America who had sided with Britain were now in dire straits, so ten thousand " United Empire Loyalists " were granted lands in Canada, others were established in New Brunswick and Nova Scotia, and several thousands found refuge in England.

Spain kept Minorca and Florida, but all the West Indian islands were handed back, except Tobago

DRAFTING THE DECLARATION OF INDEPENDENCE, L. TO R. BENJAMIN FRANKLIN, THOMAS JEFFERSON, ROBERT LIVINGSTON, JOHN ADAMS AND ROGER SHERMAN

which went to France. In Africa, France also re-covered Senegal and Goree (lost in the Seven Years War). Nothing else of importance was gained by Britain's enemies, and Britain was soon to recover her strength under William Pitt the Younger.

The loss of the American colonies was a severe shock to British pride. But, when resentment had cooled, it was realised that, though there were faults on the other side, ignorance and selfishness at home had caused the Mother Country to fail in her duty as a parent. Despite subsequent mistakes and follies, the lesson sunk in. The idea of Empire came to have a moral purpose. Trade or accident might increase the size of the British " family " overseas, but, when the colonial " children " grew up, they must be given freedom of choice to remain in the family group or to become independent. The twentieth century has seen, and is still seeing, Britain put into practice the lesson she learnt with such humiliation in George III's reign.

A lesson to Britain

GEORGE WASHINGTON
TAKES THE OATH
AS FIRST PRESIDENT
OF THE UNITED
STATES,
SURROUNDED
BY REJOICING
AMERICANS

CHAPTER 9

WILLIAM PITT THE YOUNGER

THE loss of the American colonies put an end to George III's ambition to " be a king ". Britain returned to government by a Prime Minister and a Cabinet answerable to the House of Commons, and the Whigs took office under Lord Rockingham. The leading Whigs were Lord Shelburne, Charles James Fox and Edmund Burke, the fiery Irish lawyer, but, despite their talents, they soon contrived their own downfall. Shelburne was clever but sly, Burke, the " brains " of the party, lacked the wealth and high connections for supreme office, while Fox was a brilliant enigma. A sincere lover of liberty, fearless in defending unpopular causes, Fox was also a dissolute gambler and a leading light in the hard-drinking set that surrounded the Prince of Wales.

CHARLES
JAMES FOX

In 1782 Rockingham died suddenly and the king appointed Shelburne Prime Minister. As the king expected, this so upset Fox that he and Burke refused to serve under a man they distrusted, but in his anxiety to bring Shelburne down, Fox made the mistake of his life. He formed an alliance with Lord North, on whom he had formerly poured sarcastic contempt for his conduct of the American war. With their followers, these two were able to take office together.

*A shocking
alliance*

Public opinion, hardly squeamish in the eighteenth century, was disgusted at the sight of former enemies hand-in-hand. Both were regarded with scorn, North for having lost the American colonies and Fox for rejoicing at the loss. The worst suspicions seemed to be confirmed when Fox introduced his *India Bill* of 1783.

The situation in India demanded changes, and Fox proposed that the East India Company should return to its trading, while the government (i.e. his friends and supporters) should take over the governing powers. This seemed to be a bare-faced attempt to put innumerable rich posts into the hands of the Whigs, and King George let the House of Lords know that anyone who supported the Bill must regard himself as an " enemy ".   When this move succeeded and the Bill was rejected, the king demanded the resignation of Fox and North.   They obeyed in the belief that George must soon climb down and humbly beg them to return to office.

George III takes a hand

The king did no such thing.   He appointed William Pitt to the offices of First Lord of the Treasury (the equivalent of Prime Minister) and Chancellor of the Exchequer.

Pitt was 24, a reserved, unsmiling young man who, it was said, " never was a boy ".   At Cambridge he had made few friends but had studied unusually hard, preparing himself to follow in the steps of his great father.   He had entered Parliament at 22 where, with eyes only for the highest prizes, he had scorned junior posts.   As Prime Minister, Pitt's position appeared ludicrous ; he had few supporters in the House and he had to suffer, not only the jibe

The young Mr. Pitt

> A sight to make surrounding nations stare,
> A kingdom trusted to a schoolboy's care,

but mockery for clinging to office when defeated by the Opposition.   The " schoolboy " had courage and he declared that he would not resign while he knew that he stood for the real opinion of the nation.

WILLIAM
PITT

*Pitt the Younger
comes to power*

Despite his youth and his distant autocratic manner, Pitt had assets which Fox could never rival. Cold and aloof even to his friends, nevertheless he gave an impression of steadiness and judgement. He won the goodwill of the City and the business world, which had revered his father, and he astonished everyone by refusing a sinecure worth £3000 a year. The public saw him as a brave young knight defying the hardened old tricksters in the political arena, and when Parliament was dissolved, they remembered that Pitt the Elder had saved the country and they voted for his son. Fox and North were routed, and William Pitt assumed real power. For twenty years he was to rule the country, not as a royal puppet like North, but as a Prime Minister with far wider support outside Parliament than in. The king approved of Pitt because the alternative was Fox and his terrible Whigs, who would reduce the monarch to a mere figure-head.

By nature Pitt was a reformer and a man of peace, though, in the end, he was forced to put reform on one side and to conduct a major war against revolutionary France.

Parliament was not elected by a fair system of voting, and Pitt endeavoured to abolish a number of " rotten boroughs " and to award their seats to London and to growing towns that had no Member. As a lifelong friend of Wilberforce, he also tried to restrict the Slave Trade and to improve the condition of Ireland. In these attempts he failed because of the powerful interests that were hostile to reform and, later, because the French Revolution caused men to look on liberal ideas as dangerous and unpatriotic.

In economic affairs Pitt was more successful. He came into office when Britain's finances were as low as her prestige, yet, within a few years, her spirit and prosperity were firm enough to stand the strain of a twenty years war. This recovery was largely due

WILLIAM
WILBERFORCE

to the country's growing industrial skill and to the longstanding experience of business and trade, but Pitt gave leadership and encouragement.

At Cambridge Pitt had studied Adam Smith's famous book *The Wealth of Nations*, published in 1776, that was to cut at the very roots of established notions about trade. It had long been held—and still is in some quarters—that prosperity depended upon the government's direction of trade ; in short, that the government should protect home industries by taxing foreign goods. This theory had resulted in the suppression of industries in Ireland and the colonies ; it led to the belief, among others, that farmers, manufacturers and employers should be protected from competition, even if it meant that the people at home and the customers abroad were unable to buy all that they would have wished. Adam Smith argued that this view of trade was false, since all trading was merely a form of barter that would flow more freely if governments interfered as little as possible. Prosperity in other countries would lead to greater prosperity at home because buying power would increase all round. Taxation and import duties should therefore be reduced to a minimum.

A theory of trade

When, in accordance with this theory, Pitt tried to introduce free trade with Ireland, the outcry was so great that he was forced to drop a scheme that might have changed relations with that luckless country. He was successful in putting through a commercial treaty with France (1786), and he made such heavy reductions in the taxes on tea and spirits that smuggling became unprofitable. To compensate the Exchequer, he introduced a Window Tax and, later, a tax on servants that aroused a good deal of indignation. Pitt looked into the government services and drastically reduced the number of officials and useless posts, while insisting upon an efficient way of keeping the nation's accounts.

India under Warren Hastings

While mainly preoccupied with affairs at home, Pitt was not unmindful of Britain's fallen prestige abroad, nor of the needs of her colonies. In India, more by accident than design, the East India Company found itself ruling territories too vast for a commercial company to govern efficiently. For too long, India had been a happy hunting-ground for dishonest officials who made private fortunes in the corrupt world of native politics. Clive had been succeeded by Warren Hastings, who became Governor-General in 1774, and who, by his energy and great gifts, organised a tax system, law courts and alliances with Indian princes against the warlike Mahrattas. During the American War, Hastings saved British India from the French, using some high-handed measures to obtain money for the military expenses. On his return to England, he had to stand trial for seven years for the very offences he had done so much to destroy.*

Pitt put forward an *India Act* (1784) to establish a system of government that Warren Hastings had

* Hastings was acquitted of corruption and cruelty, after a trial which cost him £70,000. He defended himself with dignity, and it was said that " he looked like a great man, and not like a bad man ".

pioneered. Business affairs remained in the hands of the East India Company, while a Board of Control appointed by the government took charge of political matters. The Board's first Governor-General was Lord Cornwallis, who established a tradition of decency and justice. He succeeded because he had power to appoint honest officials and to insist that they were properly paid.

WARREN HASTINGS IN INDIA

In Canada, a problem had arisen through the arrival of some 45,000 United Empire Loyalists from America. To escape persecution, they had migrated northwards and settled in New Brunswick and in the territory that lay west of Quebec. Since the "loyalists" were British Protestants, there could have been a clash with the French Catholics who still formed the bulk of Canada's population, and whose rights had been guaranteed by the Quebec Act. A *Canada* solution was found in Pitt's *Canada Act* (1791) which created two separate provinces, *Lower Canada*, or Quebec, with its mainly French population, and *Upper Canada*, or Ontario, where many of the British loyalists had settled. Each province had its own Assembly, with a Governor and a Council appointed by the Crown ; each therefore was free to develop in its own way until a new system was devised in Victoria's reign.

Meanwhile, a British colony came into existence in the southern hemisphere. Some years earlier, in *Australia* 1770, Captain Cook had traced the eastern coast of Australia and had claimed New South Wales for the Crown, but this great country, like New Zealand, remained unoccupied by Europeans. The loss of the

153

A CHAIN GANG
OF CONVICTS IN
AUSTRALIA

American colonies now meant that there was no convenient territory with " plantations " to receive convicts from Britain, so, as an experiment, Captain Arthur Phillip was sent out to Australia in 1788 with a party of 750 convicted persons. He landed them at *Botany Bay*, with a force of soldiers and the supplies necessary for a new settlement, which was named Sydney after the colonial secretary of that time. From this unusual beginning has grown a great Dominion. It must be remembered that many of those labelled " convicts " were men and women whose trifling offences had occurred in a society where misfortune and desperate need were ignored ; given the opportunity to settle down after they had completed their sentences, many became honest and industrious citizens of a new land.

ON BOARD A
CONVICT SHIP

CHAPTER 10

THE FRENCH REVOLUTION

THE STATE OF FRANCE

The state of France

WHEN Pitt the Younger became Prime Minister, France had long been, in many ways, the leading country in Europe. Her population was nearly three times the size of Britain's, she had flourishing industries and great agricultural riches. The magnificence of her Court, the elegance of her aristocratic society, her roads, canals, arts and manners were admired and imitated everywhere. French armies were a byword for professional skill and the French Navy had recently beaten the British in American waters. Yet France was on the verge of bankruptcy and revolution.

Compared with Britain, France was a feudal country where the pattern of social life had hardly changed since the Middle Ages. An absolute monarch, surrounded by his ministers and courtiers, ruled the country, not from Paris but from Versailles. The nobility and the higher clergy were privileged classes with little sense of responsibility towards the people beneath them, for the French aristocrat rarely lived on his estates. He was maintained at Court, along with his entire family (for the sons of a nobleman were all nobles), by the taxes and feudal dues which his steward squeezed from the tenant-farmers and peasants.

Taxation was as unjust as it was chaotic. In general, the privileged classes paid least, while the poorest peasant paid as much as 85 francs out of every 100 that he earned. Most hated of all was the *gabelle*, or salt tax, which fell most heavily upon the poor, since every person over 7 years was compelled

FRENCH ARISTOCRATIC LADIES WERE VERY ELEGANT

to buy 7 lb. of salt a year, whether he had bread to eat with it or not. Yet, so hopeless was the system, that 60,000 persons were employed in collecting the salt tax alone, and it was estimated that only one-fifth of all taxes ever reached the Treasury.

Misery of the French peasants

Famines occurred from time to time, not merely because harvests sometimes failed, but because towns and provinces had a complicated system of tolls that prevented goods from moving freely inside the country. Thus, when the harvest was bad in one part, it often proved impossible to move corn from another area where crops were plentiful.

In the country districts the peasants endured treatment that had been unknown in England since the Peasants' Revolt. Work on the lord's land and on the roads was enforced as harshly as the game-laws and feudal rights, for the French peasant, ignorant and half-starved, was regarded as little better than a brute. When at last he rose against his oppressors, he behaved with the savagery of a brute.

Yet the Revolution originated, not with the cowed peasants, but with a section of the nobility and with middle-class intellectuals. Some of the nobles who held liberal ideas wished to see a constitutional monarchy in place of the absolute rule of a king who was pulled hither and thither by corrupt courtiers and a petulant Queen. The middle-classes were prosperous and well-educated, but they resented the unjust taxation, the galling privileges of nobility and clergy, the internal customs duties that hampered trade and the vast extravagance of the Court, with its army of cooks, lackeys and grooms, its 200 carriages and 2000 horses, and its battalions of place-seekers and hangers-on.

THE FRENCH COURT
HAD 200 CARRIAGES

Writers, notably Voltaire and Rousseau, attacked the tyranny of absent landlords and wealthy bishops. They pointed to the freedom and justice that men enjoyed across the Channel in England, and they contrasted the benevolence of an ideal state with the stony-hearted indifference of monarch and aristocrat. The influence of these writers was greatly increased when Frenchmen saw, in America, that rebellion could triumph over tyranny.

THE EVENTS OF 1789

The monarch faced with this rising tide of indignation was Louis XVI. Kindly, pious and a far better man in his private life than his predecessors, Louis lacked the strength of character to put through reforms or to crush the grumbling masses under even heavier loads. Incapable of taking a strong line, he would allow events to take their own course and then, as weak men do, would put on a half-hearted show of strength that could not control the situation but merely made it worse. The mere mention of tax reform aroused such a clamour of protest from the privileged classes that his feeble efforts came to nothing and France drifted towards disaster.

The King's difficulties were increased by his isolation from his people and by the character of his wife, Marie Antoinette. Loathed because she was an Austrian and because she was known to have opposed *Marie Antoinette* various attempts at reform, the Queen became a symbol of callous oppression. Frenchmen saw, in her extravagance and even in her beauty, all that they hated in the privileged classes.

By 1789, when minister after minister had failed to solve the problem of finance because the rich refused to pay their proper share of taxation, the King agreed to summon the *States-General*, or Parliament, which

The States-General meets

had not met since 1614. After bitter dispute, it was agreed that the three " estates ", nobility, clergy and commons, should meet as one assembly, instead of in three assemblies as formerly, when the two upper classes could outvote the " third estate ". Amid great excitement the 1200 Members met at Versailles in May 1789, but in June the representatives of the people, finding blank opposition from the privileged classes, broke away and declared themselves to be the National Assembly. At a meeting in the covered Tennis Court of the Palace, they swore an oath that they would never go home until they had founded a new constitution for France.

But the members of the Assembly had little experience of how to go about the task. While Mirabeau, the ablest leader, tried to make headway, speaker after speaker rose to declaim his splendid notions for reforming a country that was now on the brink of collapse. By July, food was dearer and scarcer than ever, riots were taking place, and in Paris the hungry mob was daily growing more threatening. A Court Party urged the King to take strong measures, and his regular troops were just forming camp at Versailles when news came of a riot in the capital more serious than any before. The Revolution had begun.

The Fall of the Bastille

On July 14th 1789 a mob captured the *Bastille*, an ancient fortress on the outskirts of Paris that was supposed to be filled with victims of royal tyranny, but in fact, when the rabble broke down the doors, only seven prisoners were found inside. For centuries the Bastille had stood, like the Tower of London, for authority and the power of the ruling class. Its fall showed that there was no force to control the mob, for the Army mutinied or looked on, while exultant ruffians scrambled for loot that was dragged from the burning houses of nobles. Throughout France, the news echoed like a thunderclap ; the fall of the

MARIE ANTOINETTE

LOUIS XVI

Bastille was the end of law and order, and the hungry peasants took their revenge for centuries of oppression.

The King was powerless. Unlike Charles I, he could not count upon the affections and loyalty of half his people ; his nobles fled, his ministers were dismissed and he was forced to accept events because he could not fight them. A National Guard, composed of citizens and scoundrels too, was formed everywhere to safeguard the Revolution. In Paris, the Guard under La Fayette, hero of the American campaign, was unable to control the situation.

On October 5th the Paris mob broke out again. In pouring rain, an armed rabble, headed by almost 6000 women and children, with La Fayette and the National Guard bringing up the rear, marched to Versailles to ask the King to give them bread. At first the marchers behaved reasonably, joking with the royal bodyguards while the women dried their sodden clothes in the great Assembly Hall. At dawn the mob penetrated an inner courtyard, fired a few shots, killed some guardsmen and began howling for the King and Queen to come to Paris. Marie Antoinette went calmly on to a balcony with her two

The King and Queen taken to Paris

159

children, but though her courage appeased the crowd, there was no defying the thunderous chorus, " The King to Paris ! " That day the royal couple, the government and the Assembly were brought to Paris, accompanied by the heads of dead guardsmen swaying on pikes above the exultant procession.

THE COURSE OF THE REVOLUTION

Power passes to the mob-leaders

With the King and Queen in semi-imprisonment, and with the Assembly in Paris, power now began to pass to the political clubs and the revolutionary extremists. The King accepted the Declaration of the Rights of Man, the Assembly abolished everything —privilege, tithes, feudal dues, titles and church property, but the Members found it more difficult to build a new constitution and to restore order. While they talked, the real masters of the situation were the mob leaders.

In March 1791 Mirabeau's death put an end to all hopes of moderation, and the Assembly came to be dominated by the Paris commune (or corporation) and the violent *Jacobin Club*, whose leaders, Danton, Marat and Robespierre were republican fanatics.

Thus, in June the King attempted to escape from Paris. Though he had shown himself ready to accept almost anything, Louis XVI drew the line at surrendering his religion into the hands of State priests who had been excommunicated by the Pope. Disguised as a servant, Louis got away by coach with Marie Antoinette, and almost succeeded in reaching their friends (the émigrés) beyond the borders of France, but the fugitives were recognised at Varennes and brought back to humiliating captivity.

The *Legislative Assembly* of 1791 contained many republicans of whom the strongest party were the *Girondins*, middle-class idealists filled with lofty ideals

DANTON

A TUMBRIL CARRYING VICTIMS TO THE GUILLOTINE

of liberty and the brotherhood of man. For the moment they were fiercely determined to resist the threatened interference of foreigners by a patriotic war that would unite the nation.

The brother of Marie Antoinette was Leopold II of Austria, who had little sympathy with the French émigrés clamouring for help, but he was naturally reluctant to see his sister thrust from her throne by a barefooted rabble. With Frederick William of Prussia, Leopold issued a declaration in favour of armed intervention by the powers of Europe, whereupon France indignantly declared war on both Austria and Prussia. French troops invaded the Netherlands but were soon thrown back, and a Prussian army under the Duke of Brunswick crossed into France. *War*

Brunswick's proclamation that the King and Queen must be set at liberty aroused passionate anger in Paris where the mob, organised by Danton, stormed the Tuileries, hacked the Swiss Guard to pieces and imprisoned the royal couple in the Temple. Here, *The Paris mob*

*France becomes
a republic*

looking down at the howling mob, Marie Antoinette saw the head of her closest friend, the Princess of Lamballe, thrust up at her on a pike to the window-level. Hundreds of citizens suspected of royalist sympathies were dragged to the guillotine and executed amid scenes of savage jubilation. The *September Massacres* plunged France into the orgy of blood-thirsty terror that has become the hall-mark of revolutions. On September 21 the Legislative Assembly came to an end and a new *National Convention* abolished the monarchy and proclaimed a republic.

The Austrians and Prussia were already losing interest in the war. When the raw French troops bravely stood up to heavy gunfire at *Valmy*, the Prussian army withdrew beyond the frontier. A French army defeated the Austrians at *Jemappes* and the world was informed that France would give armed assistance to any people who rose against their rulers. Furthermore, the French government declared that it was not bound by king-made treaties, and this made it clear that the Republic would attack Austrian Belgium, would open the Scheldt to navigation and would attempt to revive Antwerp as London's rival for seaborne trade. It was equally clear that Britain

THE MOB STORMED THE TUILERIES

LOUIS XVI, ON HIS WAY TO HIS EXECUTION, SAYS GOOD-BYE TO HIS FAMILY

would fight to protect her commerce and to prevent the Low Countries from being over-run. As if to make certain of throwing away every vestige of sympathy abroad, the French government executed Louis XVI on January 21, 1793. On February 1st, war was declared on Great Britain.

THE BRITISH VIEW OF THE REVOLUTION

When news of the Revolution first reached Britain, many people had been pleased. They thought that the French would set up a constitutional monarchy like their own, and the compliment was rather flattering ; some rejoiced that liberty had come to the downtrodden peasants, and others felt that France in difficulties would no longer be a rival.

Fox supports the Revolution

Fox greeted the news of the fall of the Bastille with the remark, " How much the greatest event in the history of the world and how much the best ! " To his credit, he never changed his opinion. Writers, artists and, oddly enough, a section of the aristocracy

163

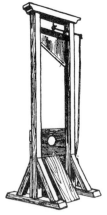

THE GUILLOTINE

found the Revolution exciting. It seemed to mark the overthrow of worn-out ideas and, to poets like Wordsworth and Shelley, to usher in an age of happiness for mankind. " Liberty ", " the rights of man " and " universal brotherhood " were wonderful words at a safe distance from the guillotine.

Pitt was more cautious, but he saw no reason why Englishmen should not remain " spectators of the strange scenes in France ", and, as late as 1792, he was prophesying peace for at least fifteen years. Only Burke, one-time Whig and friend of Fox, sounded the alarm. In his book, *Reflections on the French Revolution*, he condemned the cruelty that was taking place in the name of liberty and declared, " Revolution can only lead to bloodshed and disorder. They in turn will give place to a military tyrant." Burke's book had an enormous influence on public opinion and a war-party began to be formed.

" The Rights of Man "

Fox protested, and Thomas Paine wrote a reply, the famous *Rights of Man*, that poured scorn on Burke, upon monarchy and aristocracy everywhere. A million and a half copies of Paine's book were sold, and all over the country societies were formed to spread his ideas and to keep up correspondence with the French revolutionaries. The government could not fail to be alarmed by these activities among working-men and intellectuals who came to be known as *Radicals*.

Laws to curb the Radicals

After war broke out, laws were passed to suppress seditious opinions, and magistrates were given power to disperse meetings and to arrest Radical leaders. In 1799 the *Combination Laws* forbade workmen to combine in clubs or societies, even if their objects were only to gain better wages and conditions. These laws were later used to crush attempts to form trade unions, but at the time they seemed a small price to pay when the country was in grave danger.

THE WAR WITH REVOLUTIONARY FRANCE, 1793–1802

Pitt's war-policy was the old one of paying Britain's allies to do most of the land-fighting, while Britain kept command of the seas. In theory, this was the right policy for a sea-faring nation with a small army, but in practice it frittered away a good deal of strength in minor expeditions, especially in the West Indies, where men died like flies from fever and bad feeding. It also gave the impression in Europe that Britain was readier to pay than to fight, and that her inexhaustible store of gold could be tapped by anyone, whether they earned it or not.

Pitt's war policy

In 1793 the Allies had no outstanding military leader, and their soldiers in the ranks felt sympathy rather than enmity for the Frenchmen who had risen against their ruling-class. The French, on the other hand, became a nation in arms. Whatever the horrors of the Revolution, men felt that they had won freedom. France was fired by patriotic enthusiasm, and a million men rushed forward ready to shed their blood for their new liberty ; like Cromwell's men, they fought for their beliefs and not for pay. Soldiers of this kind were invincible against unwilling conscripts and hired men. In the revolutionary armies, promotion went to those who proved their merit and a body of excellent officers quickly came to the fore, men who had learnt their soldiering in the old army, or who had suddenly shown their military gifts and proved them on the battlefield.

Soldiers of the Revolution

The revolutionaries beat the Austrians in the Netherlands and drove a British force out of Holland, which was made an ally of France and re-named the Batavian Republic. When a British fleet entered Toulon harbour to help French Royalists in the town, a young artillery officer of the revolutionary army, named

THE TRICOLOR

NAPOLEON AT TOULON

Napoleon Bonaparte, placed his guns so skilfully that the fleet had to withdraw and leave the royalists to their fate.

British expeditions in the West Indies, along the French coast and in Corsica were no more successful and, although Lord Howe defeated the French fleet in 1794, in a battle known as *The Glorious First of June*, corn ships from America succeeded in reaching Cherbourg harbour in time to save the bread supply of France.

1795 brought such triumphs for the inspired French armies that Holland, Spain and Prussia withdrew from the war. In 1796, Bonaparte, a general at the age of 26, crushed the Austrians by a series of brilliant victories in North Italy and forced them to surrender the Netherlands by the *Treaty of Campo Formio*. The Spanish and Dutch fleets came into the service of France, but Admiral Jervis and Commodore Nelson beat the Spaniards at *Cape St. Vincent* (February, 1797). In October, after the Naval Mutinies at Spithead and Nore, Admiral Duncan destroyed most of the Dutch fleet at *Camperdown*, to make Britain safe from invasion for the time being.

Napoleon's campaign in Italy

AFFAIRS IN FRANCE

But while her soldiers were serving France with such devotion, her politicians continued to wage their cutthroat struggles for power. The Girondins were overthrown by a Jacobin group known as " *The Mountain* ", whose leaders, Danton, Marat and Robespierre turned government into a " Reign of Terror ".

" The Terror "

166

With public order and finances in confusion, with rumours everywhere of spies, riots and royalist plots, France gave way to panic. The worst of men took charge, and the *Committee of Public Safety* assumed full powers to save France by sending hundreds of citizens to the guillotine. For months no one was safe ; the accusation of " aristocrat " was enough to condemn a chamber-maid or rival politician. Leaders rose and fell ; Marat was stabbed in his bath, Danton was beheaded, and Robespierre, absolute ruler for a year, was himself executed by his enemies. In 1794 the sickening régime came to an end and was replaced by a set of men who preferred gain to blood.

MARAT

A committee of five, called the *Directory*, took over the government. Royalist supporters were on the increase, and the cry " Vive le roi " began to be heard in the streets of Paris. To keep control, the Directory called upon young Bonaparte who happened to be in Paris, temporarily unemployed. On October 4th 1795, when Paris trembled at a rising of the workers, Bonaparte proved himself to be the man of the hour. With no scruples about ordering a battery to fire into a crowd of civilians, he saved the Republic with a " whiff of grapeshot ".

The rise of Bonaparte

The Directory rewarded Bonaparte with a command. As we have seen, the unsmiling Corsican swept through Northern Italy in the most brilliant campaign of his life. But while the tiny general made treaties and plundered galleries of their treasures, without a backward glance at the men who had raised him up, his mind was already set on greater triumphs. Sending home one of his generals to root out any who remained favourable towards the monarchy, Bonaparte returned to Paris like Caesar back from the wars. The Directory shivered and looked round for fresh employment for their alarming general.

ROBESPIERRE

Bonaparte's plan   Great preparations were afoot for an invasion of England, though Duncan's destruction of the Dutch fleet had already ruined its chances. Even so, an invasion of Ireland had only failed because of bad weather, and the British Navy was kept at full stretch in the Channel and off the coast of Spain. At this stage Bonaparte revealed his own plans : he would lead an invasion, not to England, but to Egypt. He would set up a French Empire in the East and destroy the power of Britain by cutting her off from India the chief source of her wealth.

THE EGYPTIAN ADVENTURE

No one bothered to examine the flaws in this glittering prospect, least of all the Directory, which was only too glad to see Bonaparte as far from Paris as possible. In May 1798 a superb French army sailed from Toulon for Egypt, pausing on the way to capture *Malta* from the Knights of St. John.

Early in that year Admiral Jervis, now Lord St. Vincent, had managed to spare Nelson to watch Toulon with three ships. Although a storm had driven Nelson to refit, so that the French army sailed without interference, nine more warships had joined him when he learnt of Bonaparte's departure. Guessing that Egypt was the destination, Nelson hurried to Alexandria, but found no sign of the French, because of the diversion at Malta, and he sailed off to search the eastern Mediterranean. Three days later, Bonaparte landed his army at Alexandria, swiftly defeated the Mamelukes, the ruling tribesmen, at the *Battle of the Pyramids*, and claimed Egypt for France.

On August 1st Nelson arrived back off Alexandria to find the French fleet anchored across Aboukir Bay in shallow water, with protection from shore batteries and from mudbanks. Taking great risks in strange waters, Nelson attacked at dusk, ordering half his fleet to sail in single file between the French and the shore, while he himself attacked from the outside. Seamanship and tactics triumphed, for though the French fought bravely, they were caught between two fires, and by morning only 2 out of 13 ships had escaped sinking or capture. The *Battle of the Nile* gave Britain control of the Mediterranean and cut off Bonaparte from France so effectively that he could hardly receive a letter, much less men and supplies. Pitt was now able to form the *Second Coalition* of Britain, Russia, Turkey and Austria.

Nelson destroys Bonaparte's fleet in Aboukir Bay

Refusing to abandon his dream, Bonaparte marched into Palestine in order to conquer Syria and Turkey, but in his way stood the fortress of *Acre* commanding the coastal road. Admiral Sir Sydney Smith appeared offshore and landed a force of British sailors to strengthen the Turkish garrison. For sixty days Acre held out, and Bonaparte was compelled to retreat to Egypt, where he defeated another Turkish army at *Aboukir*.

The siege of Acre

News now reached Bonaparte that in France the government was tottering and that his conquests in Italy were being undone by the Allies. With only a few officers, he slipped away from Egypt, avoided the British cruisers in the Mediterranean and landed in France in October 1799. Greeted in Paris as the one man who could save the country, Bonaparte overthrew the Directory and, by a vast majority of the people's votes, became dictator of France, with the title of First Consul.

NAPOLEON BONAPARTE

Napoleon Bonaparte was a genius. Hardly more than five feet tall, the olive-skinned Corsican dominated everyone by the superhuman energy that enabled him to work all night, to browbeat his toughest marshals and to control an army, a nation and a continent. He attended to every detail of government with the same brilliant drive that he applied to his campaigns, reforming the officials, the police, the schools and the laws of France. Under his rule, a drummer-boy could become a general and a street-urchin might rise to be a minister of state, but they must serve him absolutely, with never a word of criticism. He spoke of liberty but he imposed tyranny. He said himself, " It is necessary that we should always talk of liberty, equality and justice . . . but never grant any liberty whatever." His power rested on the Grand Army, for though his marshals might secretly detest him, the soldiers adored him and believed that he was invincible. As long as he gave them victory and plunder, he could never be brought down. But the weakness of Bonaparte was the weakness of all military dictators. War made him, and to war he constantly returned to solve his problems.

Having made himself First Consul, Bonaparte magically restored the fortunes of France by breaking the Second Coalition. In 1800 he beat the Austrians at *Marengo* in Italy, and then, after Général Moreau had won another crushing victory at *Hohenlinden*, Bonaparte forced Austria to make peace.

Britain was isolated, for her ally Russia now went over to the French side. Urged on by Bonaparte, whom he vastly admired, the half-mad Tsar Paul revived the *League of Armed Neutrality*, by which Denmark, Sweden and Russia pledged themselves to resist Britain's practice of searching neutral ships to seize

NAPOLEON BONAPARTE

THE BATTLE OF THE BALTIC

enemy goods. A British fleet under Sir Hyde Parker, with Nelson as second-in-command, immediately sailed to Copenhagen to demand the surrender of the Danish Navy. The Danes refused and Nelson, taking care not to see Parker's signal to retire, sailed in and destroyed the fleet in a hard-fought engagement known as the *Battle of the Baltic* (1801).

By this time France and Britain were tired of the war. In March 1802 the *Peace of Amiens* was signed, but it proved to be no more than a truce. *A temporary peace*

Pitt had weathered the storm, but he was no longer Prime Minister when peace was made, having resigned in 1801 after a disagreement with King George III over the Irish Catholics.

Ireland had been deeply stirred by the French Revolution, which naturally appealed to a people who had suffered so long from tyranny. In 1791 a young Belfast lawyer, Wolfe Tone, formed the *Society of United Irishmen* to secure independence. French help failed to arrive only because a storm scattered the fleet carrying an army, and because, after the loss of the Dutch Navy, there were no more ships *Unrest in Ireland*

171

available. The Irish broke into armed rebellion (1798) but were soon crushed by regular troops.

The Union of 1801   These events convinced Pitt that the two countries must be united under one Parliament, and he decided to force the Union through by bribery and threats, overriding all objections by Catholics and Protestants in the belief that Ireland would benefit in the end. In 1801 the Dublin Parliament had agreed to the *Act of Union*, when an obstacle occurred that Pitt ought to have foreseen. The King refused point-blank to agree to the clause granting freedom to the Catholics, declaring that this would violate his Coronation Oath to uphold the Protestant religion. If Ireland was to be represented in the Parliament at Westminster only by Protestants, the Union was obviously a fraud, and Pitt, having made promises that he could not keep, was obliged to resign.

A TROOPER OF
THE 23RD DRAGOONS

CHAPTER II

BRITAIN AGAINST NAPOLEON

Bonaparte had signed the Treaty of Amiens so that he could put France into order, which he did with lightning speed, but he had no intention of giving up his dream to make France the greatest Power in the world. The one obstacle was Britain, the detestable " nation of shopkeepers ", whose wealth and Navy alone hindered his ambitions. Thus, war broke out again in 1803, and was to last until 1814.

In the renewed struggle both sides adopted their usual tactics. The French prepared to invade England ; Britain's Navy strove to lock up the enemy's fleets in harbour, while her ministers tried to raise yet another coalition on the Continent.

On the cliffs of Boulogne, only twenty-one miles from the English coast, Bonaparte assembled 150,000 of his finest troops. For months they drilled and practised the landings that would be made as soon as the French Navy secured control of the Channel. Thousands of barges were ready to ferry the troops across the narrow waters, but the size of the invasion army required several days in which to embark all the soldiers, guns and stores. For this, the British Navy must be utterly defeated or lured away.

Bonaparte, who now became the Emperor Napoleon while Pitt resumed the office of Prime Minister, ordered his admirals to break out of harbour.

On March 30th 1805 Admiral Villeneuve escaped from Toulon while Nelson was refitting at Sardinia. Nelson thought at first that the French had made for Egypt, but Villeneuve had joined a Spanish fleet off Cadiz (Spain had been persuaded to enter the war)

A MEDALLION OF NAPOLEON

and had sailed for the West Indies. Nelson made
furious efforts to overhaul the enemy fleet, which
turned back to Europe, and ran into Sir Robert
Calder off Cape Finisterre. Though Calder had only
fifteen ships against twenty-five, he attacked and
captured two warships. Villeneuve might have made
a dash for the Channel, but he gave up the game and
took refuge in Cadiz harbour. Nelson, bitterly disappointed, went home on leave, while Collingwood
took up the blockade of Cadiz.

Napoleon was furious with Villeneuve and raged
at the failures of his admirals, but the fact was that
the Corsican's genius did not extend to sea-warfare.
He neither understood naval affairs nor furnished his
navy with the ships and men that might have faced
the British on equal terms. Villeneuve himself wrote,
" I have bad masts, bad sails, bad officers, bad seamen and obsolete tactics." The Revolution, which
created France's magnificent army, had destroyed her
navy, because the greater number of its officers and
many of the sailors were royalists, drawn largely from
Brittany. These had long since deserted or had been
removed, and it was not possible to train good sailors
as quickly as infantrymen, especially in a country
which had never possessed a deep-rooted naval tradition.

A week after Villeneuve's retreat, Napoleon broke

MARTELLO TOWERS WERE
ERECTED ALONG THE SOUTH
COAST OF ENGLAND AS A
DEFENCE AGAINST INVASION

up his invasion camp in disgust in order to deal with what he understood—the crushing of an enemy on land. Pitt had managed to arrange " another of those creaking coalition machines "—the Third Coalition with Austria and Russia.

With terrifying precision, Napoleon struck across Europe to smash the Coalition as soon as it had formed. An Austrian army, assembling to invade France, was surrounded at *Ulm* (October 1805), Vienna was occupied and, in December, at the " Battle of the Emperors ", the main Russo-Austrian army was routed at *Austerlitz*. The Emperor Francis II had to make a humiliating peace, while the Tsar withdrew his shattered forces into Poland.

AN ENGLISH
SEAMAN

One piece of news alone relieved the gloom in England. On October 21st, the day after Ulm, Nelson destroyed the Franco-Spanish fleet at *Trafalgar*. The admiral had returned to his fleet in September, and by concealing his strength, was able to entice the enemy out of Cadiz in hope of reaching the Mediterranean. The British had fewer ships, twenty-seven to thirty-three, but more three-deckers, and there was no comparison between the officers and men of the two fleets. Nelson attacked in two columns approximately at right-angles to the enemy's strung-out line, pierced it in two places, and annihilated the centre and rear. Although it cost the life of the greatest of all admirals, Trafalgar was one of the decisive victories of history, for Napoleon could never again assemble an effective fleet, invasion was out of the question, and Britain's trade at sea, though it could still be hampered, could not be destroyed.

Trafalgar

Three months later Pitt himself was dead. The destruction of the Third Coalition proved too much for his failing health. Men said that the " Austerlitz look " never left his face and he died, already old at

*Death of Pitt,
January 1806*

forty-six, murmuring, " Oh my country ! How I
leave my country ! "

The outlook was indeed dark, and it remained so
for two and half years after Austerlitz. Napoleon
was astride Europe, where hardly a voice was raised
against him ; whole nations and emperors, it was
said, were " Bonaparte-struck ", and their armies fell
to pieces at his appearance.

In England there was no one to replace Pitt. The
so-called Ministry of All-Talents included Fox who
now had the chance to make the peace with France
that he had long been crying out for. But even Fox
found that it was easier to criticise than to come to
terms with a man bent on war. Fox died in 1806,
having achieved little in his career except the abolition of the *Slave Trade*, i.e. the shipping of slaves
from Africa in British vessels. However, the leading
Ministers, Lord Castlereagh and Canning, were
determined to continue the struggle with France.

THE CONTINENTAL SYSTEM

A FRENCH
NAVAL OFFICER

After Trafalgar, Napoleon knew that he could not
break Britain at sea, so he decided to ruin her trade
which alone enabled her to stand against the " Man
of Destiny."

The whole Continent was to be closed to British
goods. In this way, the greatest manufacturing
country in the world must be brought to bankruptcy.
Napoleon already controlled Holland, Denmark,
Belgium, France, Spain and Italy, but the ports of
North Germany were still open. Therefore, in a fortnight's campaign, Prussia was crushed. After the
Battle of Jena (October 1806), Napoleon issued the
Berlin Decree, forbidding France and all her vassal
states to trade with Britain or to admit any ship that
had called at a British port.

Russia, the last ally of England*, was the next to be brought low. After a check at *Eylau*, where he first met the stubborn quality of Russian soldiers, Napoleon won the Battle of *Friedland* (June 1807). In a sumptuous pavilion, constructed on a raft in the middle of a river, the Emperor met Tsar Alexander and compelled him to sign the *Treaty of Tilsit*. Not only did Alexander agree to join the Continental System against Britain and to bring in the smaller powers, Denmark, Sweden and Portugal, but dazzled by the Emperor's personality, he allowed himself to be called ally and friend.

" ENGLISH PLUM PUDDING MENACED "— FROM A CARICATURE OF THE TIME BY GILLRAY

The British Government had replied to the Berlin Decree with its own *Orders in Council*, claiming the right to seize neutral ships sailing to ports under French control. Now, realising what was afoot at Tilsit, the Government sent a force to seize the Danish fleet before Napoleon could use it. The bombardment of *Copenhagen* caused much bitterness abroad, just as Britain's seizure of neutral ships earned widespread hatred, and in 1812, a war with the United States of America.

Though he could do little to weaken Britain's control of the seas, Napoleon was now almost as powerful in Europe as Hitler was to be in 1941. He ruled an Empire that stretched from Southern Italy to the Baltic; the German states were parcelled together under his " protection ", Prussia was overthrown, Russia defeated, and Austria had fallen so

Europe under French rule

* Tsar Paul had been killed in a palace revolution and his successor, Alexander, remained friendly to Britain.

LUDDITES

low that her Emperor presently gave his eighteen - year - old daughter, a Hapsburg princess, to be the second wife of the Corsican, who was old enough to be her father. Napoleon made and unmade princes as he pleased. His brother Louis was king of Holland, another brother, Jerome, became king of Westphalia, a kingdom created for him in Germany, brother Lucien was a little difficult so he remained only a prince, but the eldest brother Joseph, king of Naples, was soon to be hoisted on to the throne of Spain. General Murat, who had married one of the Bonaparte sisters, then took the crown of Naples ; another sister was a princess and a third was Grand Duchess of Tuscany. The French Marshal Bernadotte was soon to become Crown Prince of Sweden and even His Holiness the Pope was a prisoner in France.

Thrones for Napoleon's family

The *Continental System* was well-nigh complete, and Napoleon could exult, " England sees her merchandise repulsed from the whole of Europe and her vessels laden with useless wealth wandering round the wide seas seeking in vain for a port to open and receive them."

Riots in Britain

There was no doubt but that Britain was hard-hit. Hundreds of ships lay idle, and prices rose as trade began to dry up. Bad harvests added to the misery of the poor and loss of business brought unemployment to many workers. There were widespread riots, especially in 1811-1812, when the *Luddites* smashed up the machines that seemed to be doing away with their labour.

178

On the other hand, Europe was suffering too. British goods and sea-borne merchandise were needed everywhere, so that smuggling became essential, even to France. Anger steadily deepened as nations saw their trade falling into ruins simply because of Napoleon's mania to break Britain at their expense.

Napoleon's mistakes

Napoleon made two fatal mistakes. He failed to realise that British sea-power could only be broken by superior fleets, and he forgot about patriotism. The Corsican of Italian descent, who always spoke French with a foreign accent, and who shuffled the crowns of Europe as he pleased, never understood the national pride of peoples who had at first welcomed the French as liberators, but now found themselves bound by a worse tyranny than before.

THE PENINSULAR WAR

When Portugal, an old ally of Britain and the one gap in the continental wall, refused to accept the Berlin Decree, Napoleon sent Marshal Junot with an army to remove the Portuguese royal family (October

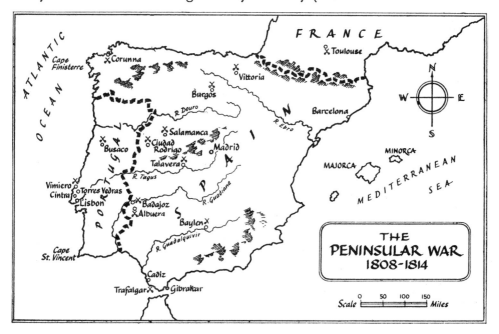

1807). Meanwhile, Napoleon enticed the Spanish king and his son across the frontier and then ordered them to abdicate in favour of his brother Joseph.

Spain and Portugal in revolt

This insult to a proud nation caused an explosion. Half a dozen provinces of Spain, calling on Britain for help, broke into revolt, and declared that they would never accept Joseph Bonaparte. In Portugal, Junot began to find that 25,000 soldiers were all too few to subdue an indignant nation.

Here, at last, was the opportunity for Britain to put her own troops into the field, and in August 1808, a force of 13,000 men was landed in Portugal under the command of Sir Arthur Wellesley (afterwards Duke of Wellington). At once he defeated Junot at *Vimiero*, and would have followed up his victory, but for the arrival of two senior officers who feebly arranged the *Convention of Cintra*, an agreement whereby Junot and his defeated troops were carried in British ships to a French port ! Such a storm of indignation burst at home that the three generals were recalled to England, and the British troops came under the command of Sir John Moore.

A MARINE

Soon afterwards, Moore was killed at *Corunna*, and Wellesley, cleared by an enquiry into the disgraceful events of Cintra, returned to Portugal. In his dry way he had informed the War Office that a British army of 30,000 troops, backed by Portuguese support, could defend the country against 100,000 Frenchmen.

Here was a new situation in Europe. Two countries, with a sea-coast that could be patrolled and supplied by English ships, had risen to arms against the Tyrant. For the first time for many a long day, French troops were seen to be anything but invincible, especially when opposed by the bayonet.

Wellesley defeats the French

In the summer of 1809 Wellesley drove Soult out of Portugal and then defeated a French army of 50,000 men at *Talavera*. For the moment, the victory only improved the morale of the British troops. Heavily reinforced, the French came on again, and compelled Wellesley to withdraw to Portugal.

Meanwhile, nearer home, an Expeditionary Force, sent to capture Antwerp where Napoleon was building *Disaster at* a fleet, failed miserably and lost nearly half its num- *Walcheren* bers from fever on the island of *Walcheren*. The soldiers were commanded by Lord Chatham and the naval force by Sir Richard Strachan (pronounced " Strawn ") and their blundering was recorded in the rhyme,

> Lord Chatham with his sword drawn,
> Was waiting for Sir Richard Strachan,
> Sir Richard longing to be at 'em,
> Was waiting for the Earl of Chatham.

WELLINGTON

Napoleon's easy victories in Spain led him to despise the difficulties of his marshals when faced by *A harsh land* an outstanding general in a harsh land. It was said that Spain was a country where a small army would be beaten and a large army would starve. Vast dry plains, ranges of jagged hills, with crumbling roads and poverty-stricken villages, made unfamiliar fighting-ground for Frenchmen trained in Germany and Italy. The country could barely feed itself, and huge armies had to transport their own food in cumbersome wagon-trains that were perpetually exposed to raiding guerillas.

But the conditions suited Arthur Wellesley, now Viscount Wellington. He regarded war as a matter of organisation, of choosing ground, of ensuring supplies, transport and lines of retreat. The poverty and

FIRING A CANNON

THE DUKE OF
WELLINGTON

Wellington's defence of Portugal

the immense spaces of Spain reminded him of India, where, he said, "If I had rice and bullocks I had men, and if I had men I knew I could beat the enemy." In Spain, it was to be mules that carried his supplies, and he kept a quarter of a million French troops and half Napoleon's generals locked up in the Peninsula for four years.

The slight, hook-nosed general with his piercing eye and sarcastic abrupt speech, was equally realistic about his men. He knew that many of his officers were incompetent boobies and he regretted in the early days that he could not send them packing ; he made no effort to win the love of his soldiers who, he said, had " all enlisted for drink ". But " the scum of the earth ", as he called them, came to have unbounded respect for their grim commander : " The sight of his long nose among us was worth ten thousand men any day," and he in his turn was to speak of them as "fine fellows " to whose " conduct, discipline and gallantry their country is so much indebted ".

In the war Wellington's tactics were clear-cut. He had to avoid being driven from the peninsula and he dared not risk a defeat, for there were critics at home in Parliament and in the War Office who kept him short of men and supplies. There was little confidence in British troops, and at the first sign of defeat there would have been an outcry to withdraw the troops. His brother and Lord Castlereagh, however, stood by him against all the pessimists.

During 1809 Wellington secured his rear by building round Lisbon the famous series of fortifications known as *The Lines of Torres Vedras*. When Masséna's enormous army advanced from Spain, Wellington fended the enemy off at *Busaco* and then took refuge inside his defence lines, with all the local population and foodstuffs from the devastated countryside. From November to March, Masséna tried to break through the mounds, ditches and gigantic earthworks that linked hills and impassable ravines, but at last he was forced to order his starving troops to retreat.

Wellington came out cautiously and followed Masséna into Spain. He captured one fortress town, but after the bloody battle of *Albuera* (1811), was unable to capture Badajoz, the key town. The freeing of Spain seemed as far off as ever, though the local guerillas were doing well in hampering the French by robbing them of supplies and perpetually watching their every move.

Suddenly, in January 1812, Wellington stormed *Ciudad Rodrigo*, the second fortress guarding the way into Spain, swept south and took *Badajoz* before Soult could rescue its defenders. The British troops showed desperate valour in storming the two strongholds, but once inside and maddened by drink and plunder, they sacked the towns with horrible violence. It was a brief lapse from discipline, for Wellington next beat " 40,000 Frenchmen in 40 minutes " at *Salamanca*. In August he was in Madrid, loaded with honours and acclaimed the saviour of Spain.

Victories in Spain

But Wellington could not stay there. His army, never more than 40,000 in the field, was not strong enough to drive the French out of Spain, so he drew Soult northwards and retired to the frontier of Portugal. When he next advanced, he was to go on right into France itself.

NAPOLEON HAD TO RETREAT FROM RUSSIA IN MID-WINTER

THE FALL OF NAPOLEON

While Napoleon was heaping abuse on his marshals for their failure in Spain, he was turning his mind to wider fields. His friendship with the Tsar had cooled. Far from obeying the Emperor's demand for stricter measures against British and American trade, Alexander declared Russian ports open. Napoleon decided to demonstrate to Europe the fate of those who disobeyed him, and in June 1812 he led the Grand Army of no less than half a million men into Russia.

It was to be more than a lesson to a foolish Tsar. After Russia had been crushed, the Emperor would go on to India; he would become Master of the World.

Napoleon attacks Russia

In his famous cloak, covering the green and scarlet uniform he loved best, and mounted on a grey, or riding in the great carriage that accompanied him everywhere, the Emperor crossed the frontier at the

184

head of the finest army that ever marched in column. *The Moscow campaign 1812* The Tsar's armies retreated into the limitless plains, burning the countryside as they went.

" Time and space are for me," said the Tsar, pointing to the map of Russia, " I am not attacking, but I shall not put down my arms as long as a foreign soldier remains on Russian soil." One hundred miles from the capital, his soldiers stood and fought bitterly at *Borodino,* where the French lost fifty generals in a day. The Russians retreated again and the French, hardly shaken, came on.

In September, Napoleon entered Moscow and found it deserted. The civilian population had left with the army, and there was no one to fight, no Tsar or city rulers to browbeat into surrender and, worse, no food.

Then the city was set on fire, perhaps by the Russians, perhaps by some drunken soldiers quarrelling at night over their wine. For weeks, Napoleon waited among the blackened ruins for peace proposals from the Tsar. No word came and, at last, the truth dawned that, since it was impossible to winter in the empty capital, the huge army must march back the way it came.

Winter closed in on the endless columns. Russian troops and the dreaded Cossack cavalry attacked incessantly along the flanks and at the rear, where Marshal Ney, " the bravest of the brave ", fought his immortal battles. The snow and the wolves did the rest. The proud army became a shambling huddle of ragged men who struggled forward with bowed heads into the snowfall. Barely 40,000 came back from the Russian plains, but by that time their Emperor had long since deserted them, racing on by sleigh and carriage to raise new armies before Europe realised the extent of the disaster.

AN ADMIRAL

But the news flew ahead and Europe rose to throw *Europe in arms against the tyrant* off the yoke. Prussia and Austria declared war on France, Sweden joined them and the German states

NAPOLEON EXTINGUISHED:
A CARICATURE OF THE
TIME

took up arms in a war of Liberation. Even so,
Napoleon was not quite done for. With all his old
energy, he twice defeated his enemies, but the new
troops were not equal to the veterans who lay in
Russia. His foes continued to mass in vast numbers,
and at *Leipzig*, the Battle of the Nations (October
1813), he was completely defeated and forced back
across the Rhine into France.

Meanwhile, in Spain, Wellington had virtually
ended the Peninsular War at *Vitoria* (June 1813).
Then he forced Soult back, yard by yard, into France
and finally defeated him at *Toulouse* (April 1814). As
Wellington rode in to the town after the battle, a
messenger approached him with news. It was great
news : Napoleon had abdicated. For the first, and
probably the only time, Wellington's staff-officers saw
the ice-cold general, the aristocrat whom nothing could
surprise or excite, put back his head and cry,
" Hurrah ! " while he snapped his fingers with delight
and kept repeating, " You don't say so, upon my
honour ! You don't say so ! "

Napoleon
surrenders

Never more brilliant than in those last desperate
months when his enemies closed in on him, Napoleon
had indeed surrendered. Paris fell, and the Emperor

went aboard an English frigate which carried him to exile on the island of Elba in the Mediterranean. The Allies, hardly able to believe that they had really snared their enemy, met at *Vienna* to re-arrange Europe. The Tsar was liberal and very high-minded, but the Congress really came together to restore the old families to their old thrones, with hardly a thought for the peoples who had seen and suffered so much.

Exile on Elba

THE HUNDRED DAYS

In March 1815 Napoleon escaped from Elba and soon entered Paris to be greeted with joy as the deliverer of France from her enemies. He immediately raised an army of 130,000 front-line troops, superbly confident of themselves, of their officers and of their brilliant commander.

The returned hero

The Allied leaders at Vienna, once they had recovered from their astonished dismay, pledged themselves to overcome Napoleon once and for all time by raising gigantic armies in Austria, Germany and Russia. For the moment, however, they could only muster a good Prussian army under Marshal Blucher, the veteran foe of France, and a mixed force of British, Dutch, Belgian and Hanoverian troops hurriedly assembled in Belgium. The Duke of Wellington came from Vienna to command this army, but many of his

THE RETURN FROM ELBA: A CARICATURE OF THE TIME

Peninsular veterans were far away in America, where they had been transferred for service in the war that had broken out in 1812.*

The Battle of Waterloo

Napoleon's aim was to occupy Brussels after he had smashed the two Allied armies. Though they were in touch with each other, Wellington and Blucher had not joined forces when the Emperor crossed the frontier on June 15th 1815 and attacked the Prussians at *Ligny*. Blucher was defeated, but his army retreated in good order under their fiery old general. More important, Blucher did not take the route which Napoleon considered must be his line of retreat; instead, he fell back upon Wavre *towards* Wellington, and not away from his ally.

Wellington had brought his army south from Brussels to *Quatre Bras*, where he withstood an attack by Ney. He now fell back to get closer to Blucher and took up his position on a ridge near the village of *Waterloo*. Blucher sent word from Wavre, 12 miles away, that he would come to assist the Duke next morning. This promise and the resolute spirit of the Prussians were unknown to Napoleon, who still believed that their shattered forces were fleeing eastwards. He sent Grouchy with 35,000 men to look after any Prussians who might be at Wavre.

Wellington placed his main army behind the ridge to protect and conceal his troops. Forward, he garrisoned

* The war of 1812–1814 with the United States was an unfortunate result of Britain's " Right of Search " when the Continental System was at its height. Each hampered the other's trade until feelings became so bitter that America declared war. Fortunately, the fighting was on a small scale and mostly at sea and on the Lakes. An American invasion of Canada failed, the town of Washington was burnt, and a British attack on New Orleans was an expensive blunder, especially as peace had already been signed. With Napoleon's fall, both sides saw sense and the *Peace of Ghent* ended the squabble. However, Wellington's soldiers could not be returned to Europe in time for Waterloo.

three strong points, the château of Hougoumont, with
its walled garden, the farm of La Haye Sainte, and
a group of farm buildings a little to the east. Thus, the
French would have to storm these outlying positions
before they could get at the main army. The Duke
had 61,000 men, of whom about 24,000 were British,
opposed to 71,000 French. NAPOLEON AT
WATERLOO AT
THE CLOSE OF
THE BATTLE

Napoleon attacked at noon on June 18th, later than
usual for him, owing to the mud and to his own
confidence : " We shall sleep tonight in Brussels," he
said to his staff, and to Soult he snapped, " Because
you have been beaten by Wellington, you think him
a great general. And I tell you that Wellington is a
bad general, that the British are bad troops and that
this will be a walk-over."

However, when the French columns charged,
Wellington met them as he had met them in Spain—
the waiting lines behind the ridge held their fire, then
came the withering volley, and then the bayonets
advanced. His forward posts were furiously assaulted
all day, but the British Guards held out among Hougoumont's broken walls : the little farm was surrounded
and thunderous attacks fell upon Wellington's centre :
" I had the infantry for some time in squares," he
wrote afterwards, " I never saw the British infantry

*The Guards hold
their position*

189

behave so well." On his horse " Copenhagen ", the Duke was everywhere coolly encouraging his sweating troops with, "There, my lads, in with you," "Ah, that's the way, lads " and " Life Guards ! I thank you ! "

By late afternoon, when the British line was still holding out but desperately tired, against incessant attacks, a force was seen approaching Napoleon's right. He assumed that this was Grouchy returning from dealing with the Prussian remnant. Instead, they were Blucher's vanguard, the first units of his main army, which had struggled all morning through *Blucher arrives* swampy ground from Wavre, urged on by their commander, " Old Marshal Forwards ", who reminded them that he had given his word to Wellington.

While Napoleon turned to meet this threat, he ordered Ney to overwhelm the British with the French cavalry. Four massed charges broke against the squares which held as though " rooted to the earth ". Even so, the Prussians were repulsed for the moment, one of Wellington's outposts was taken, and in a final effort, Napoleon ordered the Imperial Guard to attack.

In the dusk, the majestic Imperial Guard advanced, with Ney in front, at first on horseback and then walking, sword in hand. An English captain, in Maitland's Infantry Brigade, was sheltering with his men in a ditch behind a bank during the artillery bombardment that preceded the attack ; afterwards, he wrote :

THE ARC DE TRIOMPHE AT THE END OF THE NINETEENTH CENTURY

The last charge

" Suddenly the firing ceased, and as the smoke cleared away a most superb sight opened on us. A close column of Grenadiers . . . about 6000 strong . . . were seen ascending the rise, shouting ' Vive l'Empereur ! ' They continued to advance until within fifty or sixty paces of our front, when the Brigade were ordered to stand up. Whether it was from the sudden and unexpected appearance of a corps so near them, which must have seemed as starting out of the ground, or the tremendous fire we threw into them, La Garde, who had never before failed in an attack, suddenly stopped . . .

" In less than a minute above 300 were down. They now wavered, and several of the rear divisions began to draw out as if to deploy, whilst some of the men in their rear beginning to fire over the heads of those in front was so evident a proof of their confusion, that Lord Saltoun . . . halloaed out, ' Now's the time, my boys.' Immediately, the Brigade sprang forward. La Garde turned . . . we charged down the hill till we had passed the end of the orchard of Hougoumont."

As Napoleon's Guard fled, the Prussians broke through on the French right and the battle became a rout. The vengeful Prussians pursued the enemy far into the night, but the British were too tired to be moved from the field. It had been a hard struggle, " a damned serious thing," said the Duke, " the nearest run thing you ever saw in your life . . . By God ! I don't think it would have been done if I had not been there."

THE " BELLEROPHON ",
WHICH CARRIED NAPOLEON
TO EXILE IN ST. HELENA

The Emperor's final surrender

Napoleon reached Paris and then fled to the port of Rochefort, where he went aboard a British man-of-war to surrender himself to the nation which had defied him for so long. This time, there was to be no escape. Exiled to St. Helena in the South Atlantic, the ex-Emperor died there in 1821, having spent his last years weaving his own version of his glories and quarrelling with the island's unfortunate governor.

BOULAY, GRAVEUR A DIJON

NAPOLEON'S FUNERAL CORTEGE: HIS BODY WAS BROUGHT TO PARIS IN 1840 AND ENTOMBED IN LES INVALIDES

PART 4

ENGLAND AFTER WATERLOO

CHAPTER 12

TROUBLED TIMES

WITH hardly a break, England had been at war with France for 22 years. It was natural for people to believe that peace would bring the plenty that they so clearly deserved after all that they had endured.

But they were doubly wrong. Never ravaged by the Grand Army, England had suffered little compared with the continental peoples whose rulers were now arranging to take back their kingdoms on the old terms. Certainly, Britain's wealth had been poured out and her trade had been hard-hit by the Continental System. There had been much unemployment, dear bread and low wages, but there had also been big profits for those who provided the materials of war, whether great-coats, corn or field-guns.

The Navy and the Army had fought well. But in all the battles of the Peninsular War, Wellington's losses were not above 40,000 men, and when an ungrateful country turned adrift the men who had served her, the total was about 300,000 soldiers and sailors in a population of over eleven millions. Apart from drilling with the militia, the vast majority of citizens took no active part in the wars, and only a handful ever saw a Frenchman. The middle-classes had read about the fighting in newspapers, and had grumbled about Mr. Pitt's Income Tax and the rising cost of wine. But life in the country mansions and in the big farmhouses was snug and prosperous. The glossy carriages bowled down to Brighton and Bath ; the

GLOSSY CARRIAGES BOWLED DOWN TO BRIGHTON AND BATH

dandies strutted about with Beau Brummel ; ladies and gentlemen opened the latest novel by Walter Scott and were gently agitated by the poems of Wordsworth, Shelley and the scandalous Lord Byron.

As for better times, though Britain was still rich, it became evident that peace was bringing greater hardships to the poor and anxieties to the well-to-do.

After Waterloo, the government no longer needed vast amounts of food and goods for its armed forces, but the foreign trade, which might have been expected to revive, fell sadly away. Foreign governments had also ceased to buy for war ; somehow they had managed without British goods for several years and now their peoples were too poor or the markets too disorganised for a spate of buying. Thus, British employers made and sold less ; some closed down or went bankrupt ; many reduced their labour force and the numbers of unemployed rose. Thousands of *Distress after* discharged soldiers and sailors made the position *Waterloo* worse. There were, in fact, more workers than jobs, for the population had been rising steadily (in 1801, there were eleven million persons in Great Britain, in 1831, sixteen and a half million), and when children and their mothers worked all day for pennies, it was hard for a man to find a job with a decent wage.

194

The reasons for this huge increase in population *A rising*
were many. Public health was better, doctors more *population*
skilled and wages more regular in many homes ;
people married earlier and more babies survived. In
the previous century only one child out of every
four children born in London lived to reach its fifth
birthday ; a hundred years later, in 1840, three out
of four children of working-class parents survived
their babyhood, though in Manchester and Leeds
half the children still died while they were young.
Life was safer and longer ; youngsters grew up and
old people lived on past middle-age.   Somehow
children survived even in the worst conditions, in
slum houses thrown up for the factory-workers, where
clean water and sanitation were unknown, where
whole families lived in single rooms and in cellars
damp with sewage from open drains that ran down
the tracks between the houses.

The poor lived mainly on bread, and bread was *The Corn Laws*
dear. During the war, when foreign corn was scarce,
farmers had ploughed up poor land, had borrowed
money to increase their acreage and had done extremely well for a time. Now, the arrival of imported
corn and sudden falls in prices threatened them with
ruin and put labourers out of work. Parliament,
largely representing the land-owning class, quickly
passed the 1815 Corn Law, forbidding the import of

BELL'S "COMET",
THE FIRST PAS-
SENGER STEAMER
IN EUROPE, ON
THE CLYDE IN
1812

corn until the home price reached eighty shillings a quarter. This kept corn at a high price and made bread dear, but it did not give security to the small farmer, for when harvests were bad and the price of corn went very high, dealers rushed in foreign supplies and prices collapsed.

Pitt's Income Tax had been paid by the well-to-do classes who insisted that it come off, as promised, when the war was ended. But the government, needing a vast income to pay the interest on the war loans, was forced to increase taxes on almost everything that people ate, drank and wore. " Indirect " taxes of this kind always fall heaviest on the poor—if, for instance, tea is taxed, the widow pays as much on a pound of tea as a millionaire : William Cobbett, who rode about the country examining the condition of the nation, said that the workman was paying $3\frac{1}{2}$d tax on his 5d pot of beer. The value of low wages became lower still.

The Speenhamland system of helping wages out of the Poor Rate was disastrous. Rates were enormously high to help out the low wages paid by big land-owners, like the man whom Cobbett noticed in Hampshire, who had 8000 acres and had swallowed up forty farms. Unemployed labourers drifted to the towns ; some went to Canada and Australia, while others, bewildered and angry, burned down their masters' ricks and broke his windows. The magistrates naturally defended the owners of property by hanging the riot-leaders and transporting others to convict settlements.

At least, the people were free to grumble. Agitators and Radicals loudly abused the wrongs they saw on every side. Indignant journalists like Cobbett attacked the government week in and week out in their papers ; members of

A BICYCLE IN 1818
CALLED A " HOBBY-HORSE "

WILLIAM COBBETT TALKING
TO A LABOURER

" Hampden Clubs " and of " Union Clubs " in the North held meetings to demand political reform and repeal of the Corn Laws. Humbler men had their penny-a-week clubs, while the rougher sort of workmen began to march behind banners and to drill with pikes and heavy sticks. In 1816, when " Orator " *Riots* Hunt, a popular agitator, spoke in London, the revolutionary tricolour of France and caps of liberty were seen in the crowd, some of whom broke into a gunsmith's shop and the meeting became a riot with bloodshed and murder. In the Eastern Counties barns were burnt, there were riots in Lancashire, in Wales and in Staffordshire where angry workers attacked shops, ironworks and factories, while some, the " Blanketeers ", each carrying his blanket for warmth, marched towards the capital.

The ruling class was alarmed but resolute, for men like the Duke had no intention of allowing mob-rule to get the upper hand. There were no police, but the soldiers were called out ; Bow Street Runners were sent to arrest ringleaders and special constables were enrolled to protect property. On the whole, the situation was met with moderation and common sense, but occasionally, panic measures led to tragedy.

197

The Peterloo Massacre

On August 26 1819 a vast crowd, bigger than Wellington's army at Waterloo, gathered in St. Peter's Field at Manchester to listen to Orator Hunt and to demand reform. The noise, the banners and the drums so alarmed the local magistrates that a detachment of mounted yeomanry was ordered to the scene. Jostled by the crowd, the soldiers lost their heads and began to lay about them with their sabres. In the panic, eleven persons were killed and several hundreds wounded. The news of the " *Peterloo Massacre* " enraged working people and startled decent citizens who felt that this kind of thing must not be allowed to happen in England. The remarkable thing was that the casualties were so few and that the yeomen were not torn to pieces.

Almost at once the government passed the *Six Acts*. Unauthorised military training, " seditious " meetings and the keeping of arms were forbidden, and heavy penalties were imposed for " seditious libels ", with stamp duty on certain publications, in order to stop men from writing what they pleased and from publishing papers like Cobbett's " *Political Register* ".

THE POLITICAL SCENE

LORD CASTLEREAGH

The Prime Minister, Lord Liverpool, was an undistinguished leader of a Tory Cabinet, whose members generally meant well and tried to introduce mild reforms when they were not feeling alarmed about a revolution. The most powerful man in Parliament was Lord Castlereagh, who had supported Wellington through his campaigns and who now, as Foreign Secretary, was helping to settle the affairs of Europe.

THE PETERLOO MASSACRE,
A FAMOUS CARTOON
OF THE DAY

Castlereagh refused to assist the emperors of the Holy
Alliance* in their desire to crush their people's hopes
of constitutional government, but, at home, he was
looked upon as a cold, proud aristocrat, a fit subject
for the hate of the Radicals and the cruel jibes of Byron
and Shelley, who wrote, " I met Murder on the way—
He had a mask like Castlereagh."

By 1820** the government of Liverpool, Castlereagh and the die-hard Tories was detested as much
as any government in our history, and the task of *The Government*
keeping order was made more difficult by the absence *detested*

---

* The rulers of Russia, Austria and Prussia had formed the Holy
Alliance " to uphold Christian principles in government ". *Prince
Metternich*, the Austrian statesman, was the leading figure at the
Congress of Vienna ; he detested revolution and his policy was to
crush any sign of " liberalism ", i.e. of peoples having some share
in their own government.

** This was the year of the Cato Street Conspiracy, a wild plot to
murder all the Cabinet as they sat at dinner.

" THIS BLOATED
PRINCE
CHARMING "

of a leader whom men admired and of a monarch whom they respected.

George III, whose homely virtues had brought him a belated popularity, was now very old, blind and quite mad. Since 1811, his royal functions had been carried out by his son, the Prince Regent, who regarded himself as " the first gentleman of Europe ". The former friend of Fox and the Whigs almost certainly knew more about art, music and architecture than any other ruler in Europe, but by now he was anything but the elegant figure of his own imagination. He was, in fact, a pot-bellied, irritable drunkard, whose debts and immoral behaviour had been a scandal for years.

In 1820 this bloated Prince Charming, so timid that he hardly dared venture into the streets because of the jeers and brickbats that were hurled at his coach, became King George IV. Immediately, a scandal blew up that bid fair to sweep away the monarchy altogether.

As a young man George had married without his father's consent and therefore illegally a Roman Catholic lady named Mrs. Fitzherbert. Curiously enough, she loved him all her life, even though he persuaded Fox to deny the marriage so that Parliament would pay his debts. By 1795 George was again so deeply in debt that he promised his father that he would make a legal marriage if all could be settled. His father chose Caroline of Brunswick, whom the Prince married and deserted soon after the birth of a daughter, in order to return to Mrs. Fitzherbert and other loves. The luckless Princess behaved so foolishly that she was banished from royal society. Then she went abroad to enjoy herself touring Italy in a gilded carriage with a doubtful crowd of attendants and courtiers. In 1820 George IV asked his ministers to obtain him a divorce,

" The Queen's Affair "

whereupon the lady returned to contest the accusations of her husband.

The aristocracy ignored Caroline or believed her guilty, but the common people, hating George, made her a heroine and lined the streets to cheer her. A mob, decked in finery, followed her everywhere, carrying banners, breaking windows and sporting white cockades for her innocence. The Coronation had to be postponed, and the government introduced a Bill to deprive Caroline of her title and to dissolve the marriage. In the Lords a debate went on for weeks, with evidence of the most shocking nature, true or false, that was printed and read with gusto throughout the kingdom. Monarchy had sunk very low and revolution seemed certain. The mob chanted, " No Queen, no King ", Wellington took command of defence arrangements, barricades were put round the House of Lords and the Guards were near to mutiny.

Gradually, the hubbub subsided into boredom and coarse jokes. The Bill was dropped and anger faded when it was known that Caroline had accepted a pension of £50,000. In 1821 the King, tightly laced in his stays, was crowned in Westminster Abbey, from whose doors the Queen was turned away. Two weeks later she died.

BETTER TIMES

The Queen's Affair was followed by government changes that brought the beginning of a better atmosphere in the country. Castlereagh committed suicide in a fit of depression, and though George IV disliked Canning for having resigned during the persecution of Caroline, he had to accept him as Foreign Secretary.

Canning, a brilliant speaker who was never trusted

GEORGE CANNING

A " PEELER "
OF 1829

by the more aristocratic Tories, did much to establish Britain's reputation as the friend of liberty when he intervened on the side of " liberal " movements in Portugal and Spanish South America, and, above all, when he helped the Greeks in their War of Independence against the Turks (1827). Canning was joined in the Government by Robert Peel as Home Secretary, and by William Huskisson at the Board of Trade.

Peel tackled the severities of the criminal law and repealed the death penalty for over a hundred petty offences. In 1829 he founded the Metropolitan Police Force, whose indomitable " peelers " or " bobbies ", in their tall hats and tail coats, became the pattern for police forces all over the country. Huskisson steadily reduced the customs duties that had mounted during the war and the troubled peace. In this way, he helped the import of raw materials, assisted the colonies and fostered the export of manufactured goods on which Britain's prosperity depended.

These measures speeded the recovery that was gradually taking place as overseas markets began to buy again. Britain's troubles were caused by the complications which a long war added to the painful business of turning into an industrial power.

The Industrial Revolution did not occur suddenly or begin with a particular invention ; it was a process that had been going on since Tudor times, gathering pace with every improved machine, with every

PEOPLE LIVED IN SLUMS IN
OVERCROWDED INDUSTRIAL TOWNS

OVER 5000 MILES OF
RAILWAY WERE LAID
DOWN

new iron works, factory or stream-side mill. The
war increased the momentum. In 1788, Britain's
output of iron was 68,000 tons; in 1815, it was about
250,000 tons; by 1835, it totalled 1 million and in
1848, 2 million tons. Coal production had reached
16 million tons in 1815, but twenty years later it was
30 million.

Coal and iron formed the base on which industry
was founded. With mass-production of cotton goods,
woollen cloth, hardware, pottery and glass came
improvements in transport. The new roads of
Telford and Macadam chiefly affected passenger-
traffic and the speed of business dealings. The
digging of canals for heavy goods was followed by the
first railway boom. Between 1825, when the Stockton- *A railway*
Darlington line was opened, and 1848, over 5000 *boom*
miles of railway were laid down.*

Changes so rapid and irrevocable were bound to

* The more important of the early lines, all built by private enterprise, were: Liverpool and Manchester Railway (1830, when
Huskisson was accidentally killed during the opening ceremony),
London and Birmingham (1838), Great Western (1838), London
and Southampton (1840) and South Eastern (1841).

have tremendous effects on the lives of men and women who were not yet entirely divorced from the ways of the countryside. There was no plan in all this expansion of industry, no Minister or government departments to take care of sites, housing, education or public health. It was generally believed that there must be absolutely no interference with business and industry, because trade would " naturally " develop along the best and most profitable lines. It was a haphazard struggle, in which the strong and the ruthless got ahead, while their weaker rivals went under. Men such as Stephenson and Robert Owen made fortunes and treated their people better than most, but a thousand other employers fought their way upwards by hard work and grim bargaining.

Child-workers Little children worked long hours in the factories, but their parents needed the pence that they could earn ; women and girls dragged coal-trucks through passages too narrow for pit-ponies, but, said the realists, no one forced them to do so ; they needed the money. When, in 1819, Parliament limited the hours for children to 12½ a day and forbade the employment of children under nine years in certain factories, employers cried out that they would be ruined. Since there were no factory inspectors, many children went on working 15 or 16 hours a day as formerly.

Employers, mostly in the North and the Midlands, *Support for reform* hated the land-owning aristocrats who kept up the price of corn ; they themselves wanted cheap bread for their workers, not only to keep wages down, but also to enable the producers of foreign corn to buy manufactured goods from Britain. Since this state of affairs could only be remedied in Parliament, the employing class supported Reform. They resented the absurd system whereby tiny places like Old Sarum in Wiltshire sent two Members to Parliament, while Manchester, Birmingham and Leeds sent none at all.

REFORMERS

There were a few who doubted if the magnificence of the wealthy classes needed to be founded upon the miseries of the poor. Robert Owen, son of a Welsh shopkeeper, started work at the age of 9, was manager of a Manchester cotton-mill when he was 19 and made a fortune by his own efforts. At his celebrated New Lanark Mill, near Glasgow, Owen employed

CHILDREN AT WORK IN A COTTON MILL

ROBERT OWEN

LORD
SHAFTESBURY

*Beginning of
trade unions*

2000 workers, of whom 500 were pauper children from the workhouse, and he startled everyone by reducing the working day to the unheard of level of 10½ hours and by ceasing to employ children under 10 years. New Lanark became world famous, with its model village, infant school and welfare schemes, but although Owen proved that a good employer could actually prosper, he was generally regarded as something between a saint and a crank. However, through his writings and his example, Robert Owen has come to be regarded as the father of British Socialism.

Very different in background was Antony Ashley Cooper, son of the Earl of Shaftesbury, a stiff aristocratic figure whose zeal for helping the poor sprang from a deeply religious conscience and a belief that it was the duty of the governing class to provide decent working conditions. Lord Shaftesbury devoted his life to obtaining reform through Parliament, and his *Factory Acts* not only limited child labour but provided inspectors to see that the law was carried out. Similarly, it was through the passing of laws and regulations that he did so much to improve public health, education and the treatment of lunatics and children.

Meanwhile, on a less elevated level, efforts were made among the better type of workmen, known as " artisans ", to improve their conditions. The Combination Laws, passed during the French wars when sympathy with the revolutionaries was widespread, had made working-class societies illegal. Francis Place, the Radical tailor of Charing Cross, engineered the repeal of these laws in 1824, for he believed that once the workers could bargain freely with their employers, there would be no need for trade unions. He was wrong in this, for, though there was a temporary epidemic of strikes, the next ten years brought a steady growth of trade unions.

there were no factory inspectors, many children went on working 15 or 16 hours a day as formerly.

Employers, mostly in the North and the Midlands, *Support for reform* hated the land-owning aristocrats who kept up the price of corn ; they themselves wanted cheap bread for their workers, not only to keep wages down, but also to enable the producers of foreign corn to buy manufactured goods from Britain. Since this state of affairs could only be remedied in Parliament, the employing class supported Reform. They resented the absurd system whereby tiny places like Old Sarum in Wiltshire sent two Members to Parliament, while Manchester, Birmingham and Leeds sent none at all.

REFORMERS

There were a few who doubted if the magnificence of the wealthy classes needed to be founded upon the miseries of the poor. Robert Owen, son of a Welsh shopkeeper, started work at the age of 9, was manager of a Manchester cotton-mill when he was 19 and made a fortune by his own efforts. At his celebrated New Lanark Mill, near Glasgow, Owen employed

CHILDREN AT WORK IN A COTTON MILL

2000 workers, of whom 500 were pauper children from the workhouse, and he startled everyone by reducing the working day to the unheard of level of $10\frac{1}{2}$ hours and by ceasing to employ children under 10 years.   New Lanark became world famous, with its model village, infant school and welfare schemes, but although Owen proved that a good employer could actually prosper, he was generally regarded as something between a saint and a crank.   However, through his writings and his example, Robert Owen has come to be regarded as the father of British Socialism.

ROBERT OWEN

Very different in background was Antony Ashley Cooper, son of the Earl of Shaftesbury, a stiff aristocratic figure whose zeal for helping the poor sprang from a deeply religious conscience and a belief that it was the duty of the governing class to provide decent working conditions.   Lord Shaftesbury devoted his life to obtaining reform through Parliament, and his *Factory Acts* not only limited child labour but provided inspectors to see that the law was carried out.   Similarly, it was through the passing of laws and regulations that he did so much to improve public health, education and the treatment of lunatics and children.

LORD
SHAFTESBURY

Meanwhile, on a less elevated level, efforts were made among the better type of workmen, known as " artisans ", to improve their conditions.   The Combination Laws, passed during the French wars when sympathy with the revolutionaries was widespread, had made working-class societies illegal.   Francis Place, the Radical tailor of Charing Cross, engineered the repeal of these laws in 1824, for he believed that once the workers could bargain freely with their employers, there would be no need for trade unions. He was wrong in this, for, though there was a temporary epidemic of strikes, the next ten years brought a steady growth of trade unions.

Beginning of trade unions

Robert Owen's great venture, the Grand National Consolidated Trades Union, was to unite all the workers, but this alarmed the employers, and 1834 saw the case of the " Tolpuddle Martyrs ". George Loveless and a few Dorset labourers were prosecuted for taking " illegal oaths " in forming a harmless union and were sentenced to seven years' transportation. The outcry against this savage sentence was so great that the poor fellows were eventually pardoned and brought home.

ON BOARD A CONVICT SHIP

CHAPTER 13

THE REFORM BILL

*The Duke as
Prime Minister*

WHEN Lord Liverpool resigned in 1827, George IV could not avoid making George Canning Prime Minister, but Canning died within a few months and the Duke of Wellington reluctantly accepted the office, with Robert Peel as his right-hand man.

The Duke was an aristocratic Tory whose training and character made him the natural opponent of reform in any shape. He regarded politics as a campaign in which it was his duty to serve his country, to defend the Crown and the best interests of the people. Sometimes, therefore, he might have to retreat in order to save his forces from destruction, but, as he said, the best test of a general was " to know when to retreat, and to dare to do it ".

Almost at once the Duke found himself in retreat over the Test and Corporation Acts, which had been passed in Charles II's reign to prevent Dissenters from holding public offices. Broad-minded men had come to feel that it was wrong to penalise a man for his religious views and so, under pressure, the Government gave way and the Acts were repealed in 1828.

Freedom for Roman Catholics

Wellington's next retreat split the Tory party. The question of *Catholic Emancipation*, that is, the freeing of Roman Catholics from the penalties they suffered for their religion, caused feeling in Scotland and England, but in Ireland it had become a matter of life and death. The bitterness caused by the betrayal of Pitt's Act of Union had never died down. Mass-agitation, led by Daniel O'Connell, convinced Wellington and Peel that if they did not give Catholics the right to sit in Parliament, there would be civil war, and the Duke's feelings were clear on that subject : " If I could avoid . . . even a month of civil war in the country to which I am attached, I would sacrifice my life in order to do it."

Although it was too little and too late to heal the wounds inflicted upon Ireland, Catholic Emancipation was passed in 1829. Within a year, the Duke and his government had fallen.

George IV died unmourned in June 1830 and was succeeded by his 65-year-old brother, William IV, " Sailor Billy ", who at least was not unpopular. He had served at sea as a lad, had been promoted captain, and was Lord High Admiral for a short time during his brother's reign. Good-natured, tactless and fond of the bottle, William was believed to be in favour of reform.

Hardly had William IV succeeded than news came of a new revolution in France, happily bloodless. Charles X, who had succeeded Louis XVIII in 1824, was turned off his throne in favour of his cousin, Louis-Philippe, " the citizen king ". Next the Catholics of the old Austrian Netherlands, who had detested being joined to the Dutch since 1815, rose to arms, drove out the Dutch soldiers, captured Amsterdam and founded the kingdom of Belgium (1830).

To Wellington's credit he would not interfere. He

WILLIAM IV

The unpopular Duke

had done much to arrange Europe in 1815 and his arrangements were being overthrown. " There are some bitter pills to swallow," he wrote. " However, the best chance of peace is to swallow them all." Even so, these events abroad added to the Duke's unpopularity at home. He stood for the old order, and if the old order was being thrown down in France and in the Netherlands, why not in England too? The Whigs naturally opposed him and the Tories were discontented under his high-handed rule, especially since the Catholic Emancipation. With dignity Wellington resigned, and Lord Grey, leader of the Whigs, became Prime Minister.

In its long history Parliament had never represented the people, but only a section of the ruling-class, chiefly the land-owning aristocracy. It was held that property, and not people, should be represented at Westminster and, as we have seen in Chapter Five, the right to vote and the distribution of seats had hardly changed since Tudor times.

CHAIRING THE MEMBER: A HOGARTH PAINTING

Great landowners still controlled many seats in the

Commons—the Duke of Norfolk had eleven, the Earl of Lonsdale ten, and half a dozen Peers could put forty members into Parliament, because the voters in those constituencies were few in number and were tenants or employees of their Lordships. The North was badly represented, for the whole of Yorkshire returned only two members for the county, and twenty-eight for its boroughs. But a quarter of the House of Commons came from the South-West counties, where Cornwall alone sent up forty-four members, though not one of its boroughs could muster 200 voters.*

The distribution of seats in Parliament

Thus, when Lord John Russell introduced the first Reform Bill of 1831, on behalf of Grey's government, he could say, " The House of Commons . . . does not represent the people of England. A stranger who was

---

* An Almanack of 1763 gives the following figures for the House of Commons :

County	Number of Members	County	Number of Members
Cornwall	44	Buckinghamshire	14
Wiltshire	34	Norfolk	12
Devonshire	26	Surrey	14
Hampshire	26	Shropshire	12
Dorsetshire	20	Middlesex (including the City of London)	8
Sussex	20	Lancashire	14
Somerset	18	Yorkshire	30
Suffolk	16		

In this year, there were 489 Members for England, of whom 282 represented the South and the West ; Wales returned 24 Members and Scotland 45.

The Tories oppose
reform of Parlia-
ment

told that this country, every seven years, elects representatives from its population, would be very much astonished if he were to see large and opulent towns, full of enterprise and industry . . . and were then told that these towns sent no representatives to Parliament."

Yet Russell did not propose anything so revolutionary as giving the vote to every citizen. He merely wanted to abolish the rotten boroughs, to give representatives to the large towns and the vote to some of the middle-class. The Tories rightly saw that this would lead to the end of privilege and that politics would cease to be a field controlled by the aristocracy. Summoning all their strength to defend the old order, they defeated the Bill by eight votes.

The King was persuaded to dissolve Parliament. "Turn out the rogues, your Majesty!" bawled the mob as he drove to Westminster. Lighted candles stood in the windows of all who supported Reform or dared not oppose it, while crowds marched about the capital shouting, "The Bill, the whole Bill, and nothing but the Bill!" Dark windows invited brickbats, but the Duke was not the man to order candles for any mob. A few stones crashed through his windows at Hyde Park Corner, but a servant let off a blunderbuss and the crowd moved on.

THE POLITICAL UNIONS MARCH TO LONDON

THE BURNING OF BRISTOL DURING THE RIOTS

In the elections a hundred Tories lost their seats and the old Bill, hardly altered, was passed in the Commons by 345 votes to 236. In the Lords, however, though there were few as blankly opposed to it as the Duke, the Bill was defeated.

Pandemonium broke out in London and beyond. *The Bristol Riot* Peers and bishops were insulted in the streets, church bells were tolled, at Nottingham the castle was burnt and at Bristol there was a three-day riot when the prison was broken open and drunken crowds defied the soldiers who came to restore order. Everywhere, " political unions " were formed to march to London to support the government against the Lords.

A *Third Reform Bill* was passed in the Commons and sent to the Lords, where the " waverers " deserted the Duke in sufficient numbers to enable it to pass by nine votes. In Committee, however, when clause by clause was debated to the last comma, the Bill's opponents succeeded in gaining delays that might have been fatal. *The Lords delay* A plan was put forward for the King to create a large *the Bill* number of new peers who would favour the Bill and force it through the Lords. The King jibbed at this device, Grey resigned and William sent for the Duke.

Had Wellington taken office, there is little doubt that marchers would have taken the road to London.

After that, no one could have forecast the end. The Duke had openly declared the old system of electing Parliaments was the best that could be devised ; he had no sympathy for democrats and no fear of mobs, but he loved his country and regarded it as his first duty to serve his King. " We are," he remarked, " in a fine scrape, and I do not really see how we are to get out of it." No one would join him, not even Peel, in a Tory government which might try to carry a milder Bill. So the Duke advised William to recall Grey. Also, in the interests of the country, he let it be known that he would withdraw his own opposition to the Bill. In June 1832 the *Reform Act* was passed.

Wellington expected the worst : Jacobinism, revolution, civil war, for, in his view, " the government of England is destroyed ". But things were not as as bad that. 143 seats were taken from the rotten boroughs, sixty-five went to the counties (where landlords could still influence voters) and the rest to the big towns mainly in the North and the Midlands. The right to vote was extended in towns to householders who paid £10 or more in rent, in the country to owners of land worth £10, and in various classes of leaseholders. The Act did nothing at all for the working-class that had raised such a hullaballoo, for it merely made the aristocracy share its rights with the better-off middle-class.* In spirit, however, the Reform Act opened the door to further reforms.

---

* The 1832 Act gave the vote to only one man in six; working-men in some places, such as Preston, actually lost their right to vote. Bribery and influence were not ended, for, without a secret ballot, tenants were still likely to vote as their landlords wished. The new numbers of voters were England 620,000, Scotland 64,000. All the tiny boroughs were not abolished, for Thetford in Norfolk still had only 146 voters for its Member. The " £10 householder " does not sound well-to-do, but in fact his income was probably at least £150 a year, compared with the working-man's earnings of between about £20 and £50 in a year (farm labourers' wages were 7 to 9 shillings a week).

AN ERA OF REFORM

The new Parliament, with its majority of Whigs, set about its task. The first evil to be dealt with was slavery, for though the capture and transport of slaves had been abolished in 1807, slavery itself still existed in the colonies, especially in the West Indies. *The Abolition of Slavery** (1833) crowned the work of Wilberforce and Clarkson by freeing slaves in the British Empire and by compensating their owners to the tune of £20,000,000. It is ironical that this huge sum was voted by Parliament without a murmur, at a time when thousands of the country's own children lived in conditions amounting to slavery. Not a penny had been spent by the government on their schooling or recreation, until, in this same year, the miserly sum of £20,000 was granted towards the cost of building schools. This *Education Grant* was the first recognition that the cost of educating children must fall upon the State and not merely upon Church Societies and private persons.

The first reforms

Lord Shaftesbury's ceaseless battle for children was rewarded by the *Factory Act* of 1833, which improved on the Acts of 1802 and 1819. In textile factories children under 9 could not be employed at all, and those under 13 were not to work more than 9 hours a day and 48 hours in a week. Most important, Factory Inspectors were to be appointed to see that the new regulations were carried out. To everyone's astonishment, the factory owners did not go bankrupt through this interference with their " rights ".

---

* All slaves were to be freed within a year. Those in agriculture were to work for their former masters as " apprentices " until 1840, domestic slaves until 1838. In fact, the apprenticeship system ended in 1838. Supporters of the West Indian planters got the original compensation figure of £15m. raised to £20m..

A new Poor Law

The remedy for the state of affairs brought about by Speenhamland was sharp and bitter. To reduce the rates and the great class of paupers, the *Poor Law* of 1834 abolished relief for able-bodied persons except in workhouses. Rates fell, and employers were obliged to pay a living wage to their workers. Conditions gradually improved, but there was much unhappiness in the process: the poor hated the workhouse, and dreaded the approach of old age. The prospect of being separated and of going to live out their last years in prison-like conditions darkened the old age of many worthy couples.

Despite this spate of liberal reform, the Whigs were far from easy. Trade was bad again in the '30s, and taxation failed to bring in the revenue that was needed. Ireland continued to embarrass the Government, and the Radicals, feeling cheated over the Reform Act, began the *Chartist** agitation for further reforms.

In 1834 Grey retired and Lord Melbourne became Prime Minister for the next seven years, apart from one short break. A witty, easy-going man of the world, Melbourne took things quietly; men said that he roared with laughter and went off to the play when William IV suddenly dismissed him in favour of Robert Peel. But Peel and his followers, calling themselves " Conservatives " to distinguish themselves from the older diehard Tories, could not command

LORD
MELBOURNE

* The Chartists, led by Fergus O'Connor, M.P., supported the *People's Charter*. They demanded : (1) Household Suffrage, i.e. every head of household to have a vote, (2) Vote by Ballot, i.e. in secret, (3) equal electoral districts, (4) abolition of property qualification for M.P.s (so that working-men could enter Parliament), (5) payment of M.P.s, for the same reason, and (6) annual parliaments. Chartist agitation started after 1832, died down after a rising in South Wales had failed, and came to a head in 1849 when it was ridiculed out of existence. All the Chartist demands, however, except (3) and (6), have since been met.

enough support in Parliament, and Lord Melbourne returned to office.

In the early hours of June 20th 1837 William IV died at Windsor Castle. The Archbishop of Canterbury and Lord Conyngham, the Lord Chamberlain, hurried from the bedside, drove to London and arrived at 5 a.m. at Kensington Palace where the new monarch was fast asleep. She was Victoria, the eighteen-year-old daughter of George III's fourth son, Edward, Duke of Kent. When she had been roused and had put a shawl over her nightdress and her feet into slippers, the slim girl graciously received the two gentlemen who knelt and informed her that she was Queen of England.

A new reign brought new hope. There were still difficulties and hard times ahead, but things were on the mend. Even the Duke noticed that. " It is very bad," he remarked one evening at dinner, " but I consider the country on its legs again . . . yes . . . I think the country is on its legs again."

The accession of Queen Victoria

THE YOUNG
QUEEN

SUMMARY

Dates	Reigns	Events	People
1688	William & Mary (1688–1694)	Bill of Rights : Toleration Act : Mutiny Act	
1689		Siege of Londonderry ; ✕ Killiecrankie	Dundee
1690		✕ Boyne ; ✕ Beachy Head	General Mackay
1691		Treaty of Limerick	Tyrconnel
1692		Glencoe ; ✕ La Hogue	Louis XIV
1694	William III (1694–1702)	Triennial Act ; Bank of England ; Capture of Namur	Vauban Luxembourg
1695		Darien Scheme	
1697		Treaty of Ryswick	Isaac Newton
1701		Act of Settlement	James II (d. 1701)
1702	Anne (1702–1714) m. George of Denmark	War of Spanish Succession (1702–13)	
1704		✕ Blenheim ; Gibraltar ;	Rooke
1706		✕ Ramillies	Marlborough
1707		Union with Scotland	
1708		✕ Oudenarde	
1709		✕ Malplaquet	Steele, Addison
1713		Treaty of Utrecht	Vanbrugh
1714		Schism Act	Bolingbroke
1714	George I (1714–1727) m. Sophia of Brunswick		
1715		" The Fifteen " ; ✕ Sheriff-muir	Earl of Mar
1716		Septennial Act	Stanhope
1720		South Sea Bubble	Walpole
1724		Drapier's Letters	Swift, Defoe, Pope
1727	George II (1727–1760) m. Caroline of Anspach		
1730		Methodism founded	John Wesley
1736		Porteous Riots	
1739		War of Jenkins' Ear	Frederick the Great
1740		War of Austrian Succession (1740–48)	Marshal Saxe

DATES	REIGNS	EVENTS	PEOPLE
1743		✗ Dettingen ; Anson's Voyage (1740–44)	
1745		✗ Fontenoy ; " The Forty-five "	Charles Edward Stuart
1746		✗ Culloden	Dr. Johnson
1748		Treaty of Aix-la-Chapelle	Hogarth, Fielding
1751		Siege of Arcot	Clive, Dupleix
1755		✗ Fort Duquesne	Braddock
			Handel
		The Seven Years War,	William Pitt
1756		Minorca lost	Byng
1757		Klosterseven ; ✗ Plassey	
1758		Capture of Louisbourg	Amherst
1759		✗ Minden ; ✗ Quebec	Wolfe
		✗ Quiberon Bay ; ✗ Cape Lagos	Hawke, Boscawen
1760		✗ Wandewash	Eyre Coote
1763	George III		Robert Adam
	(1760–1820)	Treaty of Paris	John Wilkes
1765	*m. Charlotte of*	Stamp Act	Burke
1773	*Mecklenburg*	Boston Tea Party	Lord North
1775		War of American Independence (1775–1783)	George Washington
		✗ Lexington ; ✗ Bunker's Hill	Benjamin Franklin Warren Hastings
1776		Declaration of Independence	
1777		✗ Saratoga Springs	Captain Cook
1780		Gordon Riots	Joshua Reynolds
1781		Surrender of Yorktown	Thomas Gainsborough
1782		✗ " The Saints "	Rodney
1783		Treaty of Versailles	
1784		India Act	Pitt the Younger
1786		Trial of Warren Hastings	Wilberforce
1788		Settlement in Australia	Trevithick
1789		French Revolution	James Watt
1791		Canada Act	Charles James Fox
1793		Execution of Louis XVI	Robert Burns
		War with France (1793–1802)	Wordsworth, Coleridge

DATES	REIGNS	EVENTS	PEOPLE
1794		✕ Glorious First of June	Howe
1797		✕ Cape St. Vincent ; Naval Mutinies	Jervis Duncan
1798		✕ The Nile	Nelson
1800		✕ Marengo ; ✕ Hohen-linden	Napoleon Bonaparte
1801		✕ The Baltic ; Act of Union	Wolfe Tone
1802		Peace of Amiens	
		The Napoleonic Wars (1803–1815)	
1805		✕ Trafalgar ; ✕ Austerlitz	Canning
1806		✕ Jena ; Berlin Decrees	Castlereagh
1808		Peninsular War (1808–1814)	Wellington
1809		✕ Walcheren	
1812		Moscow campaign	Tsar Alexander I
		War with United States (1812–1814)	
1813		✕ Vitoria ; ✕ Leipzig	Blücher
1815		✕ Waterloo	
1815		Corn Laws	William Cobbett
1819		Peterloo Massacre ; The Six Acts	Constable
1820		Cato Street Conspiracy	Byron, Shelley
1820	George IV (1820–1830)	The Queen's Affair	Jane Austen, Scott
1825	m. Caroline of Brunswick	Stockton-Darlington Railway	Stephenson Huskisson
1829		Metropolitan Police Catholic Relief Act	Peel
			Robert Owen Elizabeth Fry
1830	William IV (1830–1837)		
1831	m. Adelaide of Saxe-Meiningen	First Reform Bill	Russell
1832		Great Reform Act	Grey
1833		Slavery Abolished	
		Factory Act	Shaftesbury
1834		Poor Law Amendment Act	Tolpuddle Martyrs
1837		Accession of Victoria	Melbourne

INDEX